AROUND THE LAGOON

*To Dhammica
a precious life long friend.
Christo
Nov. 2015*

ALEXANDROS PAPADIAMANDIS

AROUND THE LAGOON

REMINISCENSES TO A FRIEND

A BILINGUAL EDITION

TRANSLATED AND INTRODUCED BY

PETER MACKRIDGE

DENISE HARVEY (PUBLISHER) • LIMNI, EVIA, GREECE

First published in 2014 by Denise Harvey (Publisher)
340 05 Limni, Evia, Greece
www.deniseharveypublisher.gr

All rights reserved

Around the Lagoon (bilingual edition)
is the twenty-first publication in
THE ROMIOSYNI SERIES

Printed and bound in Greece by Alphabet S.A.

ISBN 978-960-7120-33-5

The publisher wishes to thank Domos Books,
publisher of the *Complete Works* of Alexandros Papadiamandis
(Ἅπαντα, Athens, 1981–88, 5 vols.),
edited by Nikos D. Triandaphyllopoulos,
for generously making available the original Greek text,
and the Centre for Asia Minor Studies for their kind permission to reproduce
the photographs of Skiathos taken in the 1930s by Christos Evelpidis
from the Melpo and Octave Merlier archives
published in this edition.

The drawing on the cover is by Dimitris Pikionis, *circa* 1918, from *Pikionis, Zographika*, Vol. I (Athens: Indiktos 1997), and is reproduced by kind permission of Agni Pikioni.

Also available by Alexandros Papadiamandis
The Boundless Garden: Selected Short Stories, Vol. I
The Murderess: A Social Tale

Contents

BIOGRAPHICAL NOTE 6
INTRODUCTION 7

ΟΛΟΓΥΡΑ ΣΤΗ ΛΙΜΝΗ 16
AROUND THE LAGOON 17

NOTES TO ENGLISH TRANSLATION 67
MAP OF SKIATHOS 70–1

Biographical Note

ALEXANDROS PAPADIAMANDIS was born on the Greek island of Skiathos in 1851. His father was a priest — a fact reflected in the author's surname. He received a sporadic education in Skiathos, Skopelos, Chalkida and Athens over a period of years between 1856 and 1875, when he left Athens University without completing his degree. He lived in Athens, with a profound nostalgia for his native island, for most of the period between 1873 and 1908, after which he returned to Skiathos till his death in 1911. Papadiamandis was one of the first Greeks to live from writing, though he only just earned enough to keep body and soul together. Apart from his original writings he produced fine literary translations from English and French. These included such literary classics as *Crime and Punishment* (translated from French) and *Dracula*. Between 1879 and 1884 he published three long historical novels, but he is best known and loved for his short stories, of which he published about 135, starting in 1887, and a short novel, *The Murderess* (1903). One of the explanations offered for the fact that he did not marry is that his elder sisters never married either, and that in Greece at the time it was not done for a younger brother to marry before an elder sister. Like the Greek people as a whole, Papadiamandis had an intense spiritual and emotional attachment to the Greek Orthodox Church, a devotion to its saints and to the dogmas, rituals and customs associated with it.

Introduction

'AROUND THE LAGOON', which Papadiamandis first published in two instalments in the magazine *Estia* in May 1892, is one of his most finely crafted and densely written stories. A realistic setting and a flimsy plot are used to support a wealth of highly symbolic content. The physical descriptions of the terrain in Papadiamandis's story are detailed and precise enough for us to imagine the natural setting in our mind's eye. The lagoon around which the story is set is situated immediately to the east of Skiathos town and is separated from the bay (to its south) by a strip of land, some of which is still occupied by the boatyard that Papadiamandis describes. The lagoon stands at the southern end of a narrow plain that is bordered on each side by a row of hills. It is in this plain that Alexandros Papadiamandis Airport has been built, its runway now covering the whole of the western part of the lagoon. Despite this, much of what remains of the lagoon seems to have changed little since Papadiamandis's day, and it is still a rich wildlife habitat, most of its water being supplied by the sea through a single channel (there were two channels in Papadiamandis's day) but supplemented by fresh water entering from underground sources at the northern end.

As is usual in Papadiamandis's stories, 'Around the Lagoon' combines a plot involving individual characters with descriptions of work, customs and manners practised by the whole community. Work plays a major role in this particular story, especially in the detailed and vivid descriptions of boat-building, the preparations leading up to the launch of a particular boat into the bay, and the launch itself, with its associated traditional ceremony,

but there is also an evocative scene of ploughing. In each case, as is normal in traditional Greek rural society, work is rewarded by relaxation and celebration.

The first thing that strikes the reader about the narrative is the use of the second person singular: as the subtitle informs us, the whole narrative is presented as a series of reminiscences addressed to a friend. Scholarly theses and articles on comparative literature confidently claim that second-person narrative is a modernist technique first used by the French writer Michel Butor in his novel *La Modification* (1957). In fact, Papadiamandis had already used this technique more than sixty years earlier in 'Around the Lagoon'. Although it is possible to take Papadiamandis's subtitle at face value and to imagine that the text is addressed by someone to a friend, it is perhaps more plausible to see the narrator as splitting himself into two grammatical persons (the narrator and the narratee, that is the person whom the narrator addresses), which he uses in order to talk about a single individual. In both 'Around the Lagoon' and *La Modification* there is a doubling of the self, an intense self-consciousness, but the second person also serves to invite the reader into the story, as if you or I are the main character: as Baudelaire put it, 'hypocrite Reader — my double — my brother!'[1] However, whereas in Butor's novel the narrative is a running commentary on the actions and thoughts of the narratee, in Papadiamandis's story the first person corresponds to the voice of the adult narrator and the second person refers to the child he once was. At all events, the use of the second person from the very first sentence, coupled with negative statements ('it wasn't February and there were no more narcissi') have a puzzling effect on the reader that is a far cry from conventional nineteenth-century realism.

The first sentence refers to a return after seven years, when the central character would have been aged twenty-one, but he

[1] Robert Lowell's rendering of the last line of the poem 'Au lecteur', which Baudelaire placed at the beginning of his collection *Les Fleurs du mal* (1857): 'Hypocrite lecteur, — mon semblable, — mon frère!'

is obviously narrating at a much later time than that. Although it is not specified how much time has elapsed between the events of the story and the act of narration, it may be a matter of decades. However, the author introduces what may be an anachronism at one point, which would have been topical at the time when the story was written — but also, sadly, in our own time. One of the characters is said to have been asked why he was sighing, whereupon he replied: 'I'm wondering how we're going to pay back all those millions the country owes!' Greek readers at the time were bound to be reminded of Greece's chronic inability to service the enormous foreign loans it had raised, mostly from Britain, during and after the Greek War of Independence in the 1820s. As many as eight further foreign loans were made to Greece in the period 1879–90. In May 1892, the month when 'Around the Lagoon' was first published, a new government was elected, led by Charilaos Trikoupis. Despite announcing a tough programme of cuts in public expenditure, Trikoupis failed to secure a new loan from Britain. The following year Greece defaulted on its external sovereign debt, the country was declared bankrupt and the drachma was drastically devalued. For the next sixty years Greek economic policy was controlled by an International Financial Commission.

The plot of Papadiamandis's story contains only three chief events, which take place in February and August of a single year, each of them involving three teenage children: the narratee as a fourteen-year-old child, Christodoulis, a boy of almost the same age (though he has turned fifteen by August) and a slightly older girl named Polymnia. The narrator/narratee is never named, although the fact that his grandfather is said to have been called Alexandros suggests the possibility that he bears the same name, since in Greece it is customary for children to be named after their grandparents.[1] Polymnia is named after the ancient muse of

[1] I should add, however, that the narratee's grandfather does not bear the same surname as Papadiamandis's own grandfather. We should beware of assuming that the plot of 'Around the lagoon' is purely (if at all) autobiographical.

sacred poetry and eloquence, and it is perhaps relevant to Papadiamandis's story that the muses were the daughters of Zeus and of Mnemosyne (Memory). (The etymological origin of the name is *poly-hymnia* 'many hymns'.) It is a fitting name for this beautiful and immaculately dressed girl, who is described in terms that make her seem more ethereal than earthly. Her pagan mythological name, together with the information that her late uncle was a naval commander, places her in a fairly high social class. By contrast, Christodoulis bears a name that means 'servant of Christ'. This is ironic in view of the fact that the narrator likens him to 'the last descendant of an ancient, lake-dwelling water deity, [...] forgotten for nineteen centuries, inhabiting the reeds and escaping the attention of the Christian world'. The barefoot and scantily dressed ragamuffin Christodoulis is entirely at home amid the natural world of the lagoon and its surroundings, and it is significant that there is no reference to his family; free of social ties, he roams like a hunter-gatherer, feeding himself on his catches of (sometimes illicitly acquired[1]) fish and other seafood. By contrast, the narratee's 'pedagogical servitude' to his controlling mother inhibits him from taking his shoes off and getting wet and muddy in the slimy water. Polymnia and Christodoulis, although coming from opposite ends of the social spectrum, share a natural yet mysterious grace that the sluggish, landbound lower-middle-class narratee regretfully lacks. This similarity between Polymnia and Christodoulis, combined with their social difference, encourages a mutual fascination to develop between them, from which the narratee is excluded. Both of them, however, seem to him to be the spirits that animate the place, and when he returns seven years later it seems lifeless without them.

It is relevant to the final words of the story that Christodoulis is not only the chief actor in each of the three episodes that are depicted, but his actions make a striking and positive impression

[1] Christodoulis steals fish from the lagoon, whereas Loukas pays rent to the state in return for the sole legal right to fish there.

on Polymnia. By contrast, the narratee's attempt to act in the first episode ends in humiliation; in the second he is merely an observer; while in the third there is no evidence that he even witnessed the scene; he seems to base his narrative of it on his imagination of the event. This is telling, since although the main character (as child and adult) does not act, he philosophizes in the sense that he observes himself and others, formulates his observations in language, reconstructs in his imagination the actions that he did not observe in person (together with the thoughts and feelings of the participants), and creatively assembles (re-members) all of this into a coherent whole whose meaning is greater than the sum of its parts. By means of inspiration, intuition, and spiritual and intellectual labour, the narrator has acquired the gift of literary expression, the ability to commemorate individuals now dead and to bring back to life scenes from the past. While Polymnia and Christodoulis are not presented as having an inner life, the narrator lives the 'examined life',[1] which is characterized by consciousness (and self-consciousness) in the form of observation, emotion, introspection, memory, reflection and understanding. Polymnia is what the child hero would love to possess — or at least to be favoured by — while Christodoulis is what he would like to be; yet, on a symbolic level, the narrator and Polymnia finally possess each other, she as his inspiring muse and he as her portraitist who immortalizes her in words.

The Greek text of Papadiamandis's story contains many instances of poetic wordplay that are impossible to render in translation. The most important of these involves a number of words: *limni* (lake or lagoon), *limin* (harbour, but here denoting the bay),[2] *Polymnia*, *anamniseis* (recollections) and *mnimi* (memory). On the poetic level, the similarity of these words' sounds

[1] I have in mind Plato's famous phrase, 'The unexamined life is not worth living' (*Apology*, 38a).
[2] The ancient Greek words *limnē* and *limēn* are apparently etymologically related.

brings together their meanings. Although *anamniseis* appears in the subtitle of the story and in the first sentence of the text (though nowhere else), *mnimi* appears only once, near the end of the story, in the phrase 'old Konstandis Mitzelos, of eternal memory'. The close similarity between the Greek words for 'lake' and 'memory' suggests that the lagoon is a site of memory. What the narrator remembers is a past that is so irretrievably lost as to be as good as dead, and it is no coincidence that all but one of the incidental characters who are named in the first few pages are dead by the time of the narration. But, most of all, Polymnia represents for the narrator the spirit of the lagoon that endows it with an other-worldly beauty, and Christodoulis the guardian of its natural riches, so that their disappearance by the time of the central character's subsequent visits has deprived the landscape of its sanctity, safety and beauty (and — who knows? — might one day allow it to be occupied by an international airport).

The wordplay involving *limni* transforms the lagoon from a physical to a symbolic space. As well as a site of memory, it is a site of eroticism and spirituality. The eroticism is suggested by the comparison of the nearby hillsides to 'the full breast of a maiden'[1] and by the way the shadow of the carpenter who bores holes in the timbers covers the lagoon and its surroundings, while its spirituality is indicated by the reference to the surface of the lagoon reflecting the sky (or heaven) above.

A more minor instance of wordplay is related to the flowers that Polymnia asks the narratee to pick for her. Papadiamandis uses the local word *itsia*, which denotes a kind of narcissus (*Narcissus tazetta*) resembling a daffodil with white petals and a yellow trumpet. After being thanked by Polymnia, the narrator 'is overcome by a complacent torpor that resembled the tender flower that Polymnia had sought from you'. The translation cannot reproduce the wordplay of the original: the word for 'torpor'

---

[1] It is perhaps not over-fanciful to suggest a poetic association between all these words mentioned in the previous paragraph and the Ancient Greek *hymēn*, meaning both virginity and marriage.

here (in the genitive case) is *narkis*, which is contained within the name of the flower *narkissos*. Furthermore, the word I have translated as 'complacent' is *aftareskos* (literally 'self-satisfied'); but I leave it to the reader to decide to what extent the solipsistic narrator is also narcissistic.[1]

There are two people that the narrator calls his friends. One is the narratee, whom I am treating as being the narrator's childhood self. The other is Christodoulis, whom the narrator describes as his friend no fewer than nine times. The exaggerated use of this term (like the repeated use of the adverb 'fortunately' in relation to Christodoulis's presence) is a sure sign of irony, for this friendship turns out to be purely one-sided.

The child narratee of 'Around the Lagoon' is often gently ironized by the adult narrator, who points up the gap between innocent childish fantasy and delusion and a slightly sceptical adult sense of reality — the romantic fantasy of marrying Polymnia and living happily ever after with her, and the stubborn delusion that Christodoulis is his friend. The gap between the narratee's perceptions and the narrator's is also indicated by the two occasions when, after a lengthy description of a scene, the narrator says, 'but you, friend, took no notice of these trivial things', and 'You were present at all this, my friend, yet you saw scarcely anything of it'. It is no coincidence that in both of these cases the narratee's attention is distracted by his feelings for Christodoulis and Polymnia. Most striking of all is the juxtaposition between the Greek words for love (*agapi*) and deception (*apati*) in the penultimate paragraph of the story — as though the similarity of sound between these words means that love is doomed to disappointment.

At the time when Papadiamandis's stories were first published, they were likened to the realistic fiction of other nineteenth-century European writers. By contrast, the emphasis on the inner life in 'Around the Lagoon' makes Papadiamandis's

---

[1] The narcissism of the central character is suggested by Emmanouela Kantzia in the article mentioned at the end of this introduction.

writing in this story resemble the style of later writers such as Marcel Proust and Virginia Woolf. It is perhaps no coincidence that some of the sentences in 'Around the Lagoon', in their effort to recall scenes and events that are intertwined with one another in the memory, are extremely long and complex (two of them as many as seventeen lines long each), like the apparently rambling but in reality tightly structured sentences of Proust's *A la recherche du temps perdu*, as the narrator in each case struggles to disentangle his childhood memories and impose some coherence on them.

Finally, I would like to acknowledge my debt, in revising my translation and writing my Introduction, to two recent Greek articles on 'Around the Lagoon': Yorgos Katsadorakis, 'Διαβάζοντας Παπαδιαμάντη στη λίμνη Σκιάθου', http://wwfaction.wordpress.com/2011/11/04/ologyra/ (an ecologist's examination of the Skiathos lagoon as literary setting and natural habitat); and Emmanouela Kantzia, 'Η Λίμνη του Παπαδιαμάντη', *Athens Review of Books*, October 2013, pp. 47–50, and November 2013, pp. 59–62.

Peter Mackridge
Oxford, November 2013

Around the Lagoon
Reminiscences to a Friend

Ολογυρα στη Λιμνη
Αναμνησεις προς Φιλον

Ο΄ΤΑΝ ΕΠΑΝΗΛΘΕΣ ΜΕΤΑ ΕΠΤΑ ΕΤΗ εἰς τὴν ὡραίαν τοποθεσίαν, τὴν προσφιλῆ εἰς τὰς ἀναμνήσεις σου, δὲν ἦτο Φεβρουάριος ὁ μὴν καὶ δὲν ὑπῆρχον πλέον ἴτσια νὰ μυρώνωσι τὴν ἀτμοσφαῖραν μὲ τὰς μεθυστικὰς εὐωδίας των. Ἀλλὰ δὲν ἦτο πλέον καὶ ἡ Πολύμνια ἐκεῖ, ἄλλο ἔμψυχον ὄν, ἡ μεθύσκουσα ποτὲ τὴν παιδικὴν φαντασίαν σου μὲ μόνον τῆς λευκῆς λινομετάξου ἐσθῆτός της τὸν θροῦν. Δὲν ἐσώζετο πλέον οὔτε ὁ σικυὼν τοῦ ἀγαθοῦ Παρρήση, ὁ περιβάλλων ποτὲ μὲ χλοερὸν πλαίσιον τὴν γαληνιῶσαν λίμνην, τὴν ἀντανακλῶσαν εἰς τὰ νερά της τὸ αἴθριον κυανοῦν, οὔτε κἂν ἡ καλύβα τοῦ Λούκα τοῦ Θανασούλα, ἡ βρεχομένη ἀπὸ τὸ κῦμα παρὰ τὸ στόμιον τῆς λίμνης, ὅπου οὐδεὶς ἁλιεὺς ἐτόλμα ἐντὸς βολῆς νὰ πλησιάσῃ, διότι καὶ κοιμωμένου τοῦ Λούκα, ἡ καραβίνα ἠγρύπνει παρὰ τὸ πλευρόν του, καὶ ἤκουες τότε ἔξαφνα, ἐν τῷ μέσῳ τῆς νυκτός, ξηρὸν κρότον οὐδὲν καλὸν ὑποσχόμενον εἰς τὸν τολμητίαν ὅστις θὰ ἐδοκίμαζε νὰ πλησιάσῃ ποτέ. Ἂν ἠδύνατό τις νὰ πιστεύσῃ τὰ λεγόμενα, ἡ καραβίνα αὕτη ἦτο τὸ ἀληθὲς ξυπνητήρι τοῦ ἐνοικιαστοῦ τῆς λίμνης, εἰδοποιοῦσα αὐτὸν μυστηριωδῶς διὰ κτύπου εἰς τὸν δεξιόν του ὦμον περὶ τῆς λαθραίας προσεγγίσεως βάρκας τινὸς ἐκ τοῦ λιμένος διὰ νυκτός. Διότι οἱ ὅροι τοῦ συμβολαίου ἔλεγαν ὅτι ὅλα τὰ κεφαλόπουλα καὶ τὰ καβούρια, ὅσα ἐπλησίαζαν εἰς τὴν λίμνην, ἦσαν τῆς λίμνης, ἐνῷ ὅσα ἐτόλμων νὰ ἐξέλθωσιν αὐτῆς, δὲν ἦσαν τοῦ λιμένος. Ἐφηρμόζετο δ᾽ ἐνταῦθα κατὰ πλάτος τὸ ἀξίωμα *τὰ ἐμὰ ἐμά, καὶ τὰ σὰ ἐμά.*

Ἄλλοτε κατήρχετο ἐκεῖ βόσκων τὰς ὀλίγας ἀμνάδας καὶ τὰ ἀρνία του, ὁ μπαρμπα-Γιωργός, Θεὸς σχωρέσ᾽ τον, ὁ Κοψιδάκης, ὅστις δὲν ἐφείδετο νὰ διηγῆται εἰς πάντας ὅσας ὀπτασίας ἔβλεπε (ἁγίους, ἀγγέλους, δαίμονας, τὴν κατάστασιν τῶν ψυχῶν, καὶ αὐτὴν τὴν τελευταίαν κρίσιν, ὅλα τὰ ἔβλεπεν ὁ μακαρίτης) καὶ ἅπαξ μάλιστα ἠλήθευσε περιφανῶς, ὅταν ἔπεισε

WHEN AFTER SEVEN YEARS you returned to this beautiful place, so dear to your memory, it wasn't February and there were no more narcissi to sweeten the air with their intoxicating scent. But neither was Polymnia there, that narcissus in human form who had once intoxicated your childish fancy with the mere rustle of her white dress woven from linen and silk. Nor did good Parrisis's melon-patch still survive as a green border that had once framed the calm lagoon whose waters reflected the serene blue of the sky, nor even Loukas Thanasoulas's hut, washed by the ripples near the mouth of the lagoon, where no fisherman ventured within range, since, even while Loukas slept, his carbine kept vigil at his side, and you would hear in the dead of night a sudden shot that boded no good for any impudent fellow who tried to approach. If rumours were true, this carbine was the alarm-clock for the lagoon's tenant fisherman, warning him with a mysterious tap on his right shoulder of the stealthy approach of a boat from the harbour at night. For the terms of his contract stated that all the crabs and grey mullet that approached the lagoon belonged to the lagoon, whereas those that ventured outside it did not belong to the harbour, thus applying to the full the maxim, 'all that is mine is mine, and all that is thine is mine'.*

In those days old Yorgos Kopsidakis, God rest his soul, used to bring his few ewes and lambs down to pasture there, and he never tired of telling everybody about all the visions he had seen: saints, angels, demons, the state of the souls of the dead, even the Last Judgement — all these he had seen. Once he was even proved

τοὺς πολίτας καὶ «τὸν δήμαρχο μὲ ὅλη τὴ δωδεκάδα», ὅτι ἦτο ἐπάναγκες ν' ἀνακαινίσωσιν ἐκ βάθρων τὸν ναΐσκον τοῦ Ἁγίου Γεωργίου. Καὶ προεῖπεν αὐτοῖς ὅτι, ἅμα ἀνέσκαπτον τὰ θεμέλια, ὁ Ἅγιος θὰ ἤρχετο βοηθός. Καὶ πράγματι, ὡς ἤρχισεν ἡ σκαπάνη νὰ ξεκοιλιάζῃ μετὰ δούπου τὴν γῆν καὶ νὰ στομοῦται πλήττουσα λίθους καὶ χάλικας, προέκυψαν εἰς τὸ φῶς δίδυμοι τάφοι μετὰ κιτρίνων σκελετῶν, τίς οἶδεν ἀπὸ ποίου λοιμοῦ, κατὰ τοὺς παρελθόντας αἰῶνας ἐκεῖ θαμμένων, καὶ μεταξὺ ἀδελφωμένων κοκκάλων καὶ χώματος, εὑρέθησαν περὶ τὰ ἑκατὸν ἐνετικὰ φλωρία. Ἄλλοι ἐπίστευσαν τότε τὸ θαῦμα καὶ ἄλλοι ἐξεπλάγησαν διὰ τὴν σύμπτωσιν, ἀλλὰ τὸ ὁρατὸν ἀποτέλεσμα εἶναι ὅτι ὁ ναΐσκος εὐπρεπὴς ὁπωσοῦν ἐκτίσθη. Εἰς τὸν ναΐσκον ἐκεῖνον, ὅταν ἦτο ἀκόμη παλαιὸς καὶ στενὸς καὶ μικρούτσικος, ἐκλείεσο τὸ πάλαι, ὅταν ἤθελες νὰ ἐπικαλεσθῇς τὴν βοήθειαν τοῦ Ἁγίου διὰ τοὺς πρωίμους πόνους τῆς καρδίας σου. Καὶ δὲν ἠδύνατό τις νὰ σὲ ὀνομάσῃ βέβηλον, καθόσον δὲν ἐζήτεις ἀπὸ τὸν Ἅγιον ἐγκόσμιον εὐτυχίαν, ἀλλὰ παρηγορίαν διὰ τὰς θλίψεις σου. Καὶ σὺ ἔπλεες τότε εἰς ψευδῆ ἀσφάλειαν, πεποιθὼς ὅτι κανεὶς ἄλλος δὲν σὲ ἔβλεπεν ἀπὸ τὸν Θεὸν καὶ ἀπὸ τὸν Ἅγιον· ἀλλ' ὁ νέος ἐκεῖνος ὅστις ἐφύλαγε τότε τὰ πρόβατα τοῦ μπαρμπα-Γιωργοῦ, Θεὸς σχωρέσ' τον, τοῦ Κοψιδάκη, ἂν καὶ δὲν ἦτο προικισμένος μὲ τὸ χάρισμα τῆς προφητείας καὶ τῶν ὀπτασιῶν ὡς ὁ ἀφέντης του, ὅταν σ' ἔβλεπεν ἀντικρὺ ἀπὸ τὸν λόφον, κ' ἔκλειες τὴν θύραν ἅμα ἔμβαινες εἰς τὸ ἐξωκκλήσιον, κατήρχετο γοργὰ-γοργὰ ἀπὸ τὸν λόφον μὲ τὰ τσαρουχάκια του, πατῶν εἰς τὴν γῆν τόσον μαλακὰ ὡς νὰ ἦτο ἐλαφρὸς ἀτμὸς διολισθαίνων ἐπὶ τῆς χλόης, καὶ συνέχων τὴν ἀναπνοήν του, ἐπλησίαζε σιγά-σιγὰ εἰς τὴν μικράν, μισοασβεστωμένην καὶ λαδωμένην ἀπὸ τὴν ὑπερβολικὴν εὐλάβειαν τῶν προσκυνητριῶν, ὑαλόφρακτον θυρίδα τοῦ ναΐσκου, κ' ἔβλεπε, χωρὶς νὰ τὸν βλέπῃς, τὰς μετανοίας καὶ τὰς προσευχάς σου, καὶ ἤκουε, χωρὶς νὰ τὸν ἀκούῃς, τοὺς ψιθυρισμούς σου καὶ τοὺς στεναγμούς σου. Ὦ! πόσα ἔτη παρῆλθον ἔκτοτε!

* * *

Ἐχωρίζετο ἡ λίμνη ἀπὸ τῆς θαλάσσης διὰ πλατείας λωρίδος γῆς ἀμμώδους καὶ κισηρώδους, τῆς ὁποίας μέρος ἦτο τὸ ναυπηγεῖον τῆς πόλεως καὶ μέρος ἦτο ὁ σικυὼν τοῦ Παρρήση. Κατὰ τὴν δυτικὴν ὅμως γωνίαν τῆς λωρίδος αὐτῆς, ὅπου ἤρχιζε ν' ἁπλοῦται τὸ μῆκος τοῦ λιμένος, ἡ λωρὶς αὕτη ἔβαινε στενουμένη ἕως τοῦ Ἀργύρη τοῦ Μπαρμπαπαναγιώτη τὸν ἀνεμόμυλον,

spectacularly right when he persuaded the townsfolk, including the mayor and corporation, that it was necessary to rebuild St George's from the foundations up, prophesying that when they dug down the Saint would come and assist them. And indeed, as the mattock disembowelled the earth with a dull thud, growing ever blunter as it struck stones and pebbles, it revealed twin tombs containing yellowed skeletons buried there as a result of who knows what plague during the course of the preceding centuries, and among the commingled bones and soil they found a hundred Venetian florins. Some saw this as a miracle, others were amazed at the coincidence, but the visible result was that the chapel was built rather splendidly. It was in this chapel, when it was still old and narrow and cramped, that you used to shut yourself when you wanted to invoke the Saint's aid to soothe the early pangs of your heart. No one could have accused you of irreverence, since you didn't ask the Saint for earthly happiness but for consolation for your sorrows. Meanwhile you were floating in a false sense of security, convinced that nobody else could see you but God and the Saint. Yet that young lad who looked after the sheep of old Yorgos Kopsidakis, God rest his soul, even though he wasn't endowed with the gift of prophecy and visions like his master, when he caught sight of you from the hill as you went into the chapel and closed the door behind you, used to race down in his little clogs, stepping as lightly as mist slipping over the grass, and, holding his breath, silently approach the small glass window half covered in whitewash and oil from the icon lamps as a result of the excessive piety of devout women, and watch your prayers and prostrations without being seen, and listen to your whispers and sighs without being heard. How many years have passed since then!

* * *

The lagoon was separated from the sea by a broad strip of sandy soil full of pumice, one part of which was the town's boatyard and the other Parrisis's melon-patch. At its westernmost corner, from where the harbour began to stretch out, this strip narrowed to Argyris *Barba*-Panayotis's* windmill, which, with its ceaselessly

At its westernmost corner, from where the harbour began to stretch out, this strip narrowed to Argyris Barba-Panayotis's windmill…

ὅστις μὲ τὴν ἀενάως στροφοδινουμένην κυκλοτερῆ πτέρυγά του μὲ τὰ τριγωνικὰ ἱστία, ἐφαίνετο ὡς νὰ προεκάλει τὰ ἐν τῷ λιμένι ἠγκυροβολημένα πλοῖα, λέγων πρὸς αὐτά: «Νά, ἐγὼ ἀρμενίζω καὶ στὴ στεριά!» Πόσας καὶ πόσας φορὰς ἠναγκάσθης νὰ θαλασσώσῃς, ἀφαιρῶν κάλτσες καὶ πέδιλα, ἀνασηκώνων ἕως τὸ γόνυ τὴν περισκελίδα, ἐπιμένων πεισμόνως νὰ διαβῇς τὸ ποτάμιον, ὅταν πολὺ συχνὰ ἐπήρχετο πλημμύρα καὶ ἡ θάλασσα ἐγίνετο ἓν μὲ τὸν βάλτον! Καὶ διατί δὲν ἀπεφάσιζες ν' ἀνακόψῃς τὸν δρόμον σου καὶ νὰ ἐπιστρέψῃς εἰς τὴν πόλιν; Διότι σοῦ ἐφαίνετο ὅτι κάτι ἔβλεπες, κάτι ἀπήλαυες εἰς τὸ τοπίον αὐτό, ἐνῷ ἐκείνη ἥτις τὸ ἐζωντάνευεν, εἶχε γίνει ἄφαντος πρὸ πολλοῦ. Καὶ πότε πάλιν

Then again, you preferred to take the roundabout northern route on the far side of the lagoon...

turning triangular sails, seemed to be challenging the boats anchored in the harbour, saying, 'There, I'm sailing on land!' How many times were you obliged to remove your shoes and socks and wade in, rolling your trousers up to the knee and obstinately insisting on crossing the stream when the frequent floods made the marshes one with the sea! Why didn't you abandon your walk and return to the town? Because you seemed to enjoy seeing something in this landscape, even though she who had given it life had long since disappeared. Then again, you preferred to take the roundabout northern route on the far side of the

ἐπροτίμας νὰ λάβῃς τὴν βορειοτέραν ὁδόν, τὴν περιφερῆ, ἐκεῖθεν τῆς λίμνης, διατρέχων ὅλον τὸ Κ'βούλι μὲ τοὺς ἀγροὺς καὶ μὲ τοὺς ἀμπελῶνάς του. Ἐκεῖ ἐπάτεις ἐπὶ παχείας χλόης, ὑπὸ τὴν ὁποίαν δὲν ἤξευρες πάντοτε ἂν ὑπῆρχε στερεὰ γῆ. Καὶ ἐχώνεσο ἕως τοὺς ἀστραγάλους εἰς τὸν βάλτον, ἀλλ' ἐνόμιζες τοῦτο εὐτυχίαν σου, διότι ἐφαντάζεσο πάντοτε ὅτι ἔτρεχες νὰ κόψῃς ἴτσια δι' ἐκείνην. Καὶ ὅταν ἔφθανες τέλος, μὲ τὰ ὑποδήματα βαλτωμένα καὶ τὰ περιπόδια ὑγρά, εἰς τὸν λευκὸν οἰκίσκον τοῦ μπαρμπα-Κωνσταντῆ τοῦ Μιτζέλου, καὶ τὸν ἐχαιρέτας, ἐκεῖ ποὺ ἐσκάλιζε τὰ κουκιά, φωνάζων μακρόθεν, «Καλησπέρα, μπαρμπα-Κωνσταντῆ!» κ' ἐκεῖνος σοῦ ἀπήντα μειλιχίως, «Καλῶς τὸ παιδί μου!», τότε ἠγάπας νὰ φαντάζεσαι σεαυτὸν ὡς μπαρμπα-Κωνσταντῆν, καὶ τὴν Πολύμνιαν ὡς θεια-Σινιώραν, καὶ τοὺς δύο κατὰ σαράντα ἔτη νεωτέρους, καὶ ἀνεμέτρεις ὁποία θὰ ἦτον εὐτυχία διὰ σέ, ἂν ἦτο δυνατὸν νὰ συζήσῃς μὲ τὴν ἀγαπητήν σου εἰς τὸν πάλλευκον ἐκεῖνον οἰκίσκον (τοῦ ὁποίου ὅμως ἡ ὑπερβάλλουσα λευκότης ὠφείλετο εἰς τὰ ἀκατάπαυστα ἀσβεστώματα τῆς θεια-Σινιώρας), καὶ ὁποία θὰ ἦτο ἐντρύφησις αἰσθήματος καὶ ρωμαντισμοῦ, ἐὰν διήγετε τὰς ἡμέρας μετὰ τῆς ἀγαπητῆς ἐν μέσῳ τοῦ εὐώδους καὶ χλοεροῦ ἐκείνου κήπου μὲ τὰς ροιάς, μὲ τὰς ροδωνιάς, μὲ τὰς ἀμυγδαλέας καὶ πασχαλέας, μὲ ὅλα τὰ ἐκλεκτότερα φυτὰ καὶ ἄνθη (τὰ ὁποῖα ὅμως ὠφείλοντο εἰς τοὺς ἐνδελεχεῖς κόπους τοῦ μπαρμπα-Κωνσταντῆ), παρὰ τὴν ὄχθην τῆς ὡραίας λίμνης, ὅπου ὑπῆρχεν εἷς οὐρανὸς ἐπάνω, καὶ ἄλλος οὐρανὸς ἐφαίνετο κάτω, λεῦκαι καὶ κυπάρισσοι ἀνέτεινον τὰς ὑψηλὰς κορυφάς των ἄνω, καὶ ἄλλαι λεῦκαι καὶ κυπάρισσοι ἐκρέμαντο ἀνάποδα κάτω. Καὶ ὅσαι μυριάδες ἄστρα ἐκόσμουν τὴν νύκτα λάμποντα τὸ στερέωμα, ἄλλαι τόσαι μυριάδες ἔλαμπαν τρεμοσβήνοντα κάτω εἰς τὸν πυθμένα. Καὶ καλαμῶνες σειόμενοι ὑπὸ τοῦ ἀνέμου ὕψωναν τοὺς ἀσθενεῖς καυλούς των δύο ὀργυιὰς ὑπὲρ τὸ κῦμα, καὶ βρύα καὶ λύγοι καὶ ἀσφόδελοι ἀπέζων ἐκ τοῦ ἐλέους τῆς λίμνης καὶ ἐκ τοῦ λίπους τοῦ βάλτου, κλίνοντα τὰς χθαμαλὰς κορυφάς των πρὸς τὸ ὕδωρ, ὡς ν' ἀπέδιδον εἰς τὴν λίμνην τὴν ὀφειλομένην εὐγνώμονα ὑπόκλισιν. Καὶ ἀντικρὺ ὑψοῦτο ὁ λιμὴν μὲ τὰς χλοερὰς ὄχθας του ὁλόγυρα, τὰς ἐξαπλούσας εἰς τὸν ἥλιον τὰς πρασινιζούσας κλιτῦς των, ὡς εὔκολπα στήθη παρθένου ἀναδίδοντα ζωὴν καὶ σφρῖγος εἰς τὴν πλάσιν. Δένδρα ἐκόσμουν εὐπαρύφως τὰς ὄχθας τὰς ὀρεινὰς καὶ τὰς ἀμμώδεις, καὶ ἄλλα δένδρα φυτευμένα ἐν τῇ θαλάσσῃ ἐστόλιζον τὸ κῦμα καὶ τοὺς αἰγιαλούς, τὰ ἱστία μὲ τὰ ἐξάρτιά των. Καὶ εἰς τὸ βάθος ἐφαίνοντο πρὸς βορρᾶν

lagoon, crossing the whole of Kivouli with its fields and vineyards. There you walked on lush grass, not always certain that there was firm ground underneath, and you would sink into the marsh up to your ankles, but you thought yourself fortunate because you always imagined you were running to pick narcissi for her. And when, your shoes muddy and your socks soaked through, you finally reached old Konstandis Mitzelos's white cottage and you greeted him from afar as he hoed his broad beans with a 'Good evening, Uncle Konstandis!', and he replied in his affable manner, 'Well, hello, my boy!', you loved to imagine yourself as old Konstandis, and Polymnia as Aunt Siniora, forty years younger, and you imagined how happy you would be if it were possible to live together with your beloved in that white cottage (whose rather excessive whiteness was due to Aunt Siniora's incessant whitewashing), and how delightfully romantic it would be if you spent your days with your beloved in the midst of that fragrant and luxuriant garden, with its pomegranates, its rose-bushes, its almond-trees and lilacs, with all those exquisite trees and flowers (which, however, were due to old Konstandis's assiduous labours), at the edge of the beautiful lagoon, where there was one sky above and another seemingly below, and poplars and cypresses extended their tall tips upwards, while other poplars and cypresses hung topsy-turvy. And when myriads of stars adorned the night, shining in the firmament, as many myriads twinkled down in the depths. Reeds shaken by the wind reared their fragile stems two fathoms above the surface, and mosses and chaste-trees and asphodels lived on the mercy of the lagoon and on the slime of the marsh, inclining their low heads towards the water as if bowing in gratitude. Opposite rose the grassy banks of the harbour, presenting their green slopes to the sun like the full breasts of a maiden offering life and vigour to the whole of creation. Trees adorned the undulating sandy margins of the shore, while other trees planted in the sea — the masts with their sails — embellished the waters of the harbour.

In the distance, towards the north, appeared the two rows of

τεμνόμεναι αἱ δύο τῶν λόφων σειραί, αἱ περιβάλλουσαι ἔνθεν καὶ ἔνθεν τὸν μακρὸν ἀλλ' εὐσύνοπτον εἰς τὸ βλέμμα κάμπον, ἡ μία ἡ ἀνατολική, ὑψηλή, ἐγγυτέρα εἰς τὸν θεατήν, ἐπιστεφομένη ἀπὸ τὸ καλύβι τοῦ μπαρμπα-Γιωργιοῦ, Θεὸς σχωρέσ' τον, τοῦ Κοψιδάκη, ὅπου ὄχι ἅπαξ ἑώρτασες τὴν Πρωτομαγιάν, παιδίον, μὲ γάλα καὶ μὲ ὀβελίαν ἀμνὸν καὶ μὲ στεφάνους καὶ μὲ λούλουδα, ὅταν ἔζη ὁ πρὸς μητρὸς πάππος σου, ὁ μπάρμπ' Ἀλέξανδρος, Θεὸς σχωρέσ' τον, ὁ Καρονιάρης, ὅστις ἠγάπα νὰ ἑορτάζῃ μεγαλοπρεπῶς τὴν Πρωτομαγιάν, χορηγὸς αὐτὸς ὄχι μόνον δι' ὅλους τοὺς υἱούς, τὰς θυγατέρας καὶ τὰ ἐγγόνια του, ἀλλὰ καὶ διὰ τὰ ἀναδεξίμια του καὶ τοὺς κουμπάρους του καὶ διὰ τὰς κόρας τῶν κολληγισσῶν του ἀκόμη, τὰς ὁποίας ἑπταέτης ἤδη δὲν ὤκνεις νὰ ἐρωτεύεσαι, φανταζόμενος ὅτι τρέχεις κατόπιν αὐτῶν εἰς τοὺς ὁρμίσκους, ἐκεῖ ὅπου ἐλεύκαιναν τὰς ὀθόνας, καὶ ὅτι κρύπτεσαι μαζί των εἰς τὰ ἄντρα, τὰ πατούμενα ὑπὸ τῆς θαλάσσης, ἀφριζούσης ὑπὸ τὴν πνοὴν τοῦ Βορρᾶ, ὀνειροπολῶν τὴν εὐτυχίαν εἰς τοὺς λευκοὺς καὶ γλαφυροὺς κόλπους, μὲ τὰς ὁλοβροχίνους καὶ βυσσινόχρους τραχηλιάς, καὶ εἰς τὰς κυανόφλεβας καὶ τορνευτὰς ὠλένας μὲ τὰς μακρὰς καὶ κεντητὰς χειρίδάς των. Πρώιμα ὄνειρα νεότητος ἀνυπομόνου, ὡς ἡ ἀμυγδαλῆ ἡ ἀνθοῦσα τὸν Ἰανουάριον!

Ἡ ἄλλη, ἡ δυτικὴ λοφιά, ἦτο ἡ Πλατάνα, ἀπωτέρα εἰς τὸν θεατήν, ὑπτία, ἀνακεκλιμένη, βαθμηδὸν ἀνέρπουσα πρὸς τὰς ὑψηλοτέρας κορυφάς, ἧς τὴν ὑπώρειαν περικαλλῶς κοσμεῖ ὁ Πύργος τοῦ Μετοχίου, μὲ τὸν ὡραῖον ναΐσκον τοῦ Ἁγίου Ἰωάννου τοῦ Θεολόγου. Ὅλα αὐτὰ τὰ ἔβλεπες ἀντικρύ σου ὡς τελείαν εἰκόνα ἀριστοτέχνου ἀληθῶς, ἐκεῖθεν τῆς λίμνης ἀπὸ τὸν λευκὸν οἰκίσκον τοῦ μπαρμπα-Κωνσταντῆ τοῦ Μιτζέλου, καθὼς καὶ ἀπὸ τὸ ναυπηγεῖον, τὸ ὁποῖον ἐφαίνετο ἀπέναντι, ἐντεῦθεν τῆς λίμνης.

* * *

Ὅλη ἡ μακρὰ καὶ πλατεῖα ἀμμουδιὰ ἡ ἁπλουμένη μεταξὺ τῆς λίμνης καὶ τοῦ λιμένος, δὲν εἶχεν οὐδὲ ἕνα κόκκον ἄμμου ἀμιγῆ ἀπὸ πριονίδια, οὐδὲ ἕνα χάλικα ἐλεύθερον ἀπὸ τὴν γειτονίαν πελεκουδίου. Πόσα δάση ἀγριοξύλων μετεμορφώθησαν ἐνταῦθα, ἀπὸ ἀμνημονεύτων χρόνων, εἰς σκάφας μὲ κατάρτια ὑψηλά, μὲ μυριάδας ὀργυιῶν σχοινίων καὶ πανίων, καὶ πόσαι τοιαῦται σκάφαι θὰ ἐκοιμῶντο τώρα τὸν αἰώνιον ὕπνον εἰς τὰ βάθη τῆς Μεσογείου ἢ τοῦ Εὐξείνου! Δύο τοιοῦτοι σκελετοὶ ἐφαίνοντο σήμερον κείμενοι ἐπὶ τὴν μίαν πλευράν, εἰς τὰ ρηχά, ἀντικρύ

hills that rose on either side of the plain which, though extensive, could be easily taken in at one glance. The eastern hills were high, closer to the spectator, crowned by the hut of old Yorgos Kopsidakis, God rest his soul, where more than once you celebrated May Day as a child, with milk, and lamb on the spit, and garlands of flowers, when your maternal grandfather, old Alexandros Karoniaris, God rest his soul, was alive, who loved to celebrate May Day in grand style, entertaining not only all his sons, his daughters and his grandchildren, but his godchildren and his *koumbaroi** and even the daughters of his share-croppers, with whom, at the early age of seven, you were not slow to fall in love, imagining yourself running after them to the little coves where they washed the sheets and hiding with them in caves invaded by the sea that foamed with the north wind's breath, and daydreaming of the delight within their elegant white bodices, their cherry-red silk jabots, their well-turned, blue-veined forearms in their long embroidered sleeves. Precocious dreams of impetuous youth, like an almond-tree blossoming in January!

The other range of hills, to the west, was Platana, more distant from the spectator, lying supine but sloping slightly upwards towards the peaks at whose foot stood the fine tower of Metochi, with the beautiful chapel of St John the Theologian. You could see all this, like the perfect painting of a true master, beyond the lagoon, from old Konstandis Mitzelos's little white house or from the boatyard which was visible on this side of the lagoon.

* * *

On the whole of the long, broad beach that stretched between the lagoon and the harbour there was as much sawdust as there was sand, no pebble without a chip of wood lying next to it. How many forests had been transformed here from time immemorial into tall-masted vessels, with thousands of fathoms of ropes and sails, and how many of those vessels must now be sleeping eternally in the depths of the Mediterranean or the Black Sea! That day two such skeletons could be seen lying on

τοῦ ναυπηγείου, μὲ τὰς σκωληκοβρώτους καὶ μαυρισμένας σανίδας των, μὲ τὰ σκουριασμένα καρφία των, καὶ τὰ διέχοντα στραβόξυλα γυμνὰ μαδερίων, δι' ὧν διέρρεεν ἐλευθέρως ἡ θάλασσα, ἐφαίνοντο θλιβερῶς μειδιῶντα, μὲ ὀδόντας ἄνευ χειλέων, ὡς νὰ ᾠκτειρον βλέποντα ἐκ τοῦ σύνεγγυς τὴν τόσην μανιώδη μέριμναν καὶ μεταλλευτικότητα τῶν ἀνθρώπων. Πόσαι χεῖρες ἀνθρώπων πυρετωδῶς ἐργασθεῖσαι ἄλλοτε ἐδῶ δὲν ἔκειντο ξηραὶ εἰς τὰ βάθη τῆς γῆς, πόσαι κεφαλαί, τόσον ἔχουσαι ἐγκέφαλον, ὅσος θὰ ἤρκει, καθ' ἃ ἔλεγε γηραιὸς ναυτικός, «διὰ νὰ παλαμίσῃ τις ἕνα καράβι ὁλόκληρον», δὲν ἔθρεψαν ἀδηφάγα κήτη εἰς τὸν βυθὸν τοῦ πόντου! Καὶ ὅμως ὁ γέρων ἐκεῖνος θαλασσινός, μὲ τὴν πικρὰν εἰρωνείαν, εἶχε χάσει ἀρτίως τὸ πλοῖον καὶ τοὺς δύο υἱούς του ἀπὸ τρικυμίαν παρὰ τὸν Μαλέαν, καὶ τώρα, μὲ τὰ γεράματά του, καὶ μὲ τὸν τρίτον του υἱόν, ἐπαιδεύετο νὰ ναυπηγήσῃ ἄλλο πλοῖον μεγαλύτερον, ἔρημος τῶν κυριωτέρων βοηθῶν του! Οὕτως ἡ ἀνάγκη τοῦ βίου καὶ ἡ συνήθεια δεσπόζουσι τῶν ἀνθρωπίνων πραγμάτων! Δι' ἐκεῖνον τὸ νέον τοῦτο πλοῖον ἴσως νὰ ἦτο, ἂν ὄχι ἱκανοποίησις, τοὐλάχιστον παρηγορία διὰ τὸ γῆρας! Καὶ οὕτω θὰ ἐξηκολούθει νὰ διάγῃ τὰς τελευταίας ἡμέρας του, ὁ γηραιὸς θαλάσσιος λύκος, ἑωσότου θὰ ἤρχετο ἴσως ἡμέρα καθ' ἣν ἡ θάλασσα, τὸ μέγιστον τοῦτο θηρίον τὸ ὁποῖον ἐπιμόνως προεκάλει, θὰ τὸν ἀνέρριπτεν ἐξεγειρομένη ἀπὸ τῶν κόλπων της ἕως τὸ στερέωμα, ὡς λέγει ὁ Βάυρων, καὶ θὰ τὸν ἔπεμπεν ὀλολύζοντα «εἰς τοὺς θεούς του», ἀπορρίπτουσα αὐτὸν ὀπίσω εἰς τὴν γῆν. «Ἐκεῖ ἂς κεῖται!» There let him lay!

Κ' ἐξηκολούθουν διαρκῶς νὰ ναυπηγῶσι πλοῖα, καὶ ἡ τέχνη ἐτελειοποιεῖτο καὶ τὸ ἐμπόριον ηὔξανε. Πᾶς ὅστις ἤθελε νὰ ναυπηγήσῃ εἶχε πρόθυμον σύμβουλον τὸν καπετὰν Δημήτρη τὸν Κασσανδριανό, μὲ τὴν μακράν του τσιμπούκαν, μὲ τὸ ἠλέκτρινον στόμιον, ὅστις εἶχεν ἰδεῖ καὶ ἀκούσει πολλὰ εἰς τὴν ζωήν του, ὁ μακαρίτης. Τὰς ἡμέρας τοῦ γήρατός του τὰς ἐδαπάνα παριστάμενος θεατὴς τῶν ναυπηγουμένων πλοίων, ἐρχόμενος κατὰ πᾶσαν ἑσπέραν μὲ τὴν τσιμπούκαν του, μὲ τὴν μακρὰν καπνοσακκούλαν του κρεμαμένην ἐπὶ τοῦ τσοχίνου ἐπανωβράκου, διὰ νὰ καμαρώσῃ τοὺς κόπους καὶ τὰς ἐλπίδας τῶν ἄλλων, καὶ παρηγορηθῇ διότι, πεισθεὶς εἰς τὰς ἀπαιτήσεις τῶν υἱῶν του, ἰσχυριζομένων ὅτι ἦτο παρὰ πολὺ γέρων, εἶχε παραχωρήσει αὐτοῖς τὴν πλοιαρχίαν. «Σὰ θὰ κάμετε τὸ σταυρό σας νὰ κόψετε τὸν κερεστέ, παιδιά, νὰ κοιτάξετε καλὰ πόσω ἡμέρῳ θὰ εἶναι τὸ φεγγάρι... Κι ὄντας θὰ σκαρώσετε, μὲ τὸ καλό, νὰ ξετάζετε

their sides in the shallows opposite the boatyard, with blackened, worm-eaten timbers and rusted nails, while their gaping ribs, stripped of their planking, through which the sea ebbed and flowed freely, seemed to be smiling sorrowfully, with lipless teeth, out of pity at the spectacle of such frenzied human industry and inventiveness. How many human hands that had once worked feverishly here now lay withered in the depths of the earth, how many heads containing enough brains, in the words of an old sailor, 'to tar a whole ship', had nourished the insatiable monsters of the deep! Yet that same old seaman, known for his bitter sarcasm, had recently lost his own boat and his two sons in a storm near Cape Malea, and now, in his old age, with the assistance of his third son but bereft of his chief helpers, was struggling to build a larger one. Thus are human affairs dominated by habit and material necessity! Perhaps for him this new boat was a source, if not of satisfaction, at least of consolation for his old age. In this way the old sea-dog would continue to live his last days until the hour came when the sea, that greatest of monsters, which he had persistently challenged, would arise and spurn him from her bosom to the skies, as Byron puts it, sending him shivering and howling 'to his Gods', and dashing him again to earth: 'There let him lay'!*

They went on incessantly building boats, and their skill came closer to perfection, and trade increased. Anyone who wanted to build a boat would have found an eager adviser in the late Captain Dimitris Kassandrianos, with his long pipe with its amber mouthpiece, who had seen and heard many things in his life. He spent his old age watching the boat-building, coming every evening with his pipe, his long tobacco-pouch hanging from his thick woollen breeches, to take pride in the hopes and labours of others and to console himself for having been persuaded to relinquish the command of his boat to his sons, who maintained that he was too old. 'When you cross yourselves before cutting the timber, boys, look carefully to see how many days old the moon is. And when you begin to build, with God's help, check to see where the star is.

On the whole of the long, broad beach that stretched between the lagoon and the harbour there was as much sawdust as there was sand, no pebble without a chip of wood lying next to it. [p. 25]

ποῦ εἶναι ὁ ἀστέρας... *Βάρδα μπένε, νὰ μὴ σκαρώσετε μουδὲ νὰ τὸ ρίξετε στὸ γιαλὸ τὴν ἡμέρα ποὺ εἶναι λιοτρόπι...»* Καὶ ἔδιδε βραδύγλωσσος πολυτίμους ὁδηγίας εἰς τὸν πλοίαρχον, ὡς καὶ εἰς τὸν πρωτομάστορην, περὶ πάντων τῶν συντελούντων εἰς τὴν ἐπιτυχῆ ναυπήγησιν ὡς καὶ τὴν εὐόδωσιν καὶ προκοπὴν τοῦ πλοίου. Ὅστις δὲν τὸν ἤκουε, τόσον χειρότερα δι' αὐτόν! Νεωτερισταί τινες πλοίαρχοι ἐδοκίμασαν νὰ τὸν παρακούσουν, καὶ ὑπέφεραν σκληρῶς.

* * *

The blows of the sledgehammer drowned out the rhythmical rasping of the saw, the knocking of the adze overpowered the thumping of the wooden mallet... [p. 31]

Take care not to build a boat or launch it at the solstice.'* In his lisping voice he would give valuable instructions to the captain, and even to the master builder, concerning all matters that contributed to the successful construction as well as to the launching and sailing of the boat. If anyone refused to listen to him, so much the worse for them! Certain innovators among the ships' captains had tried ignoring him, and they had suffered cruelly.

* * *

Ἐνθυμεῖσαι, ὑπῆρχαν τότε τρία μεγάλα σκάφη πλησίον ἀλλήλων ναυπηγούμενα, ὑπὸ τὸν αὐτὸν ἀρχιναυπηγόν. Θαυμάσιος ἄνθρωπος! Πῶς ἠδύνατο νὰ ἐπαρκῇ καὶ εἰς τὰ τρία, τρέχων ἀπὸ σκάφης εἰς σκάφην, μ' ἕνα πῆχυν εἰς τὴν χεῖρα, μὲ μίαν στάθμην καὶ μ' ἓν σκέπαρνον ἀπὸ τοῦ αὐχένος κρεμάμενον μὲ τὴν λαβὴν ἐπὶ τοῦ στέρνου. Καὶ ὁποία στρατιὰ ἀνθρώπων ἐτέλει ὑπὸ τὰς διαταγάς του! Ὁ πλοίαρχος, οἱ βοηθοί του, οἱ πριονισταί, οἱ πελεκηταί, οἱ μαραγκοὶ καὶ οἱ καλαφάται! Δὲν ἔλειπαν καὶ οἱ Γύφτοι, οἵτινες εἶχον ἱδρύσει προχείρως ἀνὰ μίαν καλύβην ὄπισθεν ἑνὸς ἑκάστου τῶν σκαφῶν. Καὶ μὲ τὴν κάμινον πλήρη ἀνθράκων, μὲ τοὺς φυσητῆρας, μὲ τοὺς ἄκμονας, μὲ τοὺς ραιστῆρας καὶ τὰς βαρείας σφύρας των, ἔκοπταν, ἔκοπταν μεγάλα καρφία, *τζαβέτες*. Ὁποῖος φοβερὸς θόρυβος! Οἱ κτύποι τοῦ ραιστῆρος ἔπνιγον τὸν ἔρρυθμον τριγμὸν τοῦ πρίονος, ὁ κρότος τοῦ σκεπάρνου ἐκάλυπτε τὸν δοῦπον τῆς ξυλίνης ματσόλας, δι' ἧς ἐκτύπα τὸ στυππεῖον ὁ καλαφάτης, καὶ ὑπὲρ πάντας τοὺς ἄλλους κρότους ἐδέσποζεν ὁ βαρὺς ροῖβδος τοῦ πελωρίου ραιστῆρος, δι' οὗ ἐνέπηγον τὰ χονδρὰ καρφία καὶ τοὺς ξυλίνους ἥλους, *τὲς καβίλιες*, εἰς τὰς στρογγύλας πλευρὰς τοῦ κολοσσαίου σκάφους. Καὶ ὑψηλός, μεγαλόκορμος ἀνήρ, μὲ ὀρθὰς τὰς πλάτας, μὲ τὸ κόκκινον πλατὺ ζωνάρι συνέχον τὴν μακρὰν σέλλαν τοῦ βρακίου ὑπὸ τοὺς βουβῶνάς του, εἶχεν ἀναβῆ, ὁ δαιμόνιος, ὑψηλὰ ἐπὶ τῆς κωπαστῆς, καὶ ὁ ἴσκιος του μακρός, ὑπὸ τὰς τελευταίας ἀκτῖνας τοῦ δύοντος ἡλίου, ἐμεγεθύνετο τεραστίως, τῶν μὲν σκελῶν πιπτόντων ἐντεῦθεν τῆς λίμνης ἐπὶ τῶν φυτῶν τοῦ σικυῶνος, τοῦ δὲ κορμοῦ ἀορίστως κυμαινομένου ἐπὶ τοῦ ὕδατος, καὶ τῆς κεφαλῆς ζωγραφουμένης μεγαλοπρεπῶς πέραν τῆς λίμνης, πρὸς ἀνατολάς, εἰς τὴν ὑπώρειαν τοῦ βουνοῦ. Οὗτος ἦτο ὁ *πουργοτζῆς*, ἔργον ἔχων τὸ ν' ἀνοίγῃ τρύπες. Ὑπερμέγεθες πισσωμένον ζεμπίλιον, κείμενον κάπου, ἀνάμεσα εἰς δύο *βουβά*, μεγάλα ξύλα, ὑπὸ τὴν πρύμνην, ἦτο γεμᾶτον ἀπὸ τριβέλια διαφόρων μεγεθῶν, ἕως τρεῖς δωδεκάδας, ὧν τὸ μὲν μικρότερον θὰ ἦτο ἕως δύο σπιθαμῶν, τὸ δὲ μέγιστον, βαρύ, ὀγκῶδες, ἦτο σχεδὸν ἴσον μὲ τὸ ἀνάστημα τοῦ κατόχου του. Τὴν στιγμὴν ταύτην ἐχειρίζετο ἀκριβῶς ἓν τῶν μεγίστων τρυπανίων, καὶ ἔκυπτεν, ὁ θαυμάσιος, ἐπὶ τῆς κωπαστῆς, αἰωρούμενος ὡς σχοινοβάτης, καὶ ἤνοιγε βαθεῖαν κάθετον ὀπὴν εἰς μίαν τῶν πλευρῶν τοῦ σκάφους. Ὢ τῆς ἀκαταληψίας!

At that time, you remember, there were three large craft being built next to one another under the supervision of the same master shipbuilder. What a wonderful man he was! How was he able to cope with all three ships, running from one to another with his cubit measuring-stick in his hand, his plumb line, and his adze hanging from his neck with its handle across his chest? And what an army of men laboured under his command: the captain, his assistants, the sawyers, the hewers, the carpenters, and the caulkers! The gypsy blacksmiths were there too, having erected a makeshift hut behind each ship. With their furnace full of charcoal, their bellows, anvils, sledgehammers and other smaller hammers, they were forging great bolts. What a fearful din! The blows of the sledgehammer drowned out the rhythmical rasping of the saw, the knocking of the adze overpowered the thumping of the wooden mallet with which the caulker was banging in the oakum, while all the other sounds were dominated by the resounding bang of the huge sledgehammer with which the thick iron bolts and wooden pegs were being driven into the curved sides of the colossal hull. One tall, strapping man with a straight back, his breeches hitched up under his groin with a broad red sash, had ingeniously climbed way up on to the gunwale, and his shadow was immensely elongated in the last rays of the setting sun, the legs falling on the melon-plants growing on this side of the lagoon, the torso faintly undulating on the surface of the water, and the head outlined magnificently beyond the lagoon, at the foot of the mountain towards the east. This was the driller, whose task was to bore holes in the timbers. A huge basket lined with pitch, lying between two great unhewn timbers beneath the stern, was full of drill-bits of various sizes, some three dozen of them, of which the smallest was about two spans in length, while the biggest, bulky and heavy, was almost the same height as its owner. At that very moment this wonderful man was handling one of the largest drills and, leaning over the gunwale and hanging in mid-air like a tightrope-walker, was drilling a deep vertical hole in the side of the hull. How he did it was incomprehensible!

* * *

Ἀλλ' ὁ ἥλιος ἐκρύβη ἤδη εἰς τὴν κορυφὴν τοῦ ὑψηλοῦ πετρώδους βουνοῦ, καὶ ὁ ἴσκιος τοῦ *πουργοτζῆ* διεγράφη καὶ αὐτὸς *ἀπὸ τὴν ἐπιφάνειαν τοῦ ὕδατος καὶ ἀπὸ τὸν ἄμμον τῆς παραλίας*. Οἱ μαστόροι, καθὼς καὶ οἱ πολλοὶ ἐπισκέπται, οἱ περιπατηταὶ τῆς ἑσπέρας, οἵτινες ἤρχοντο νὰ συγκοπιάζωσι καὶ αὐτοὶ μὲ τὸ βλέμμα εἰς τοὺς ἱδρῶτας τῶν ἄλλων, κ' ἐνίοτε νὰ τοὺς χασομερῶσι μὲ τὰς ἀκαίρους ἐρωτήσεις των, διασκελίσαντες τὰ παντοῦ ἐσκορπισμένα ἀνὰ τὸ ναυπηγεῖον *βουβά*, δοκοὺς καὶ στραβόξυλα, συνήχθησαν ὅλοι ἐν συγκεχυμένῳ βόμβῳ, περὶ τὴν μικρὰν καλύβην τοῦ πλοιάρχου, ἥτις ἦτο πλήρης τάκων καὶ τεμαχίων ξύλου καὶ σπυρίδων μὲ ἐργαλεῖα καί τινων ἐνδυμάτων καὶ κλινοσκεπασμάτων, διὰ νὰ πίωσιν ὅλοι τὸ *τσίπουρο*, ἀπὸ μεγάλην χιλιάρικην φιάλην, μὲ τὸ αὐτὸ ποτήριον ὅλοι. Μόνος ὁ πελώριος καραβόσκυλος, ὁ προσδεδεμένος μὲ στερεὰν ἅλυσιν ἔξω τῆς καλύβης, ὄπισθεν τῆς πρύμνης τοῦ μεγάλου σκάφους, ἐξέπεμπεν ἀπειλητικὸν ὑπόκωφον γρυλισμόν, ὡς νὰ διέκρινεν αὐτὸς μόνος τὸν βόμβον τῶν κηφήνων ἀπὸ τοῦ βόμβου τῶν μελισσῶν, κ' ἐφαίνετο, ἂν τοῦ τὸ ἐπέτρεπαν, ἕτοιμος νὰ ἐφορμήσῃ. Ἀλλ' ὁ πλοίαρχος, ὁ καπετὰν Γιωργάκης, ὅστις ἐφαίνετο κάπως μορφωμένος, μὲ τοὺς μακροὺς ἀγκιστροειδεῖς ξανθοὺς μύστακάς του, τὸ ἡλιοκαὲς πρόσωπον καὶ τὸ μικρὸν ἀνάστημα, διὰ μονοσυλλάβων ἀνέκοπτε τὴν ὁρμήν του. «Πίσω, Τσοῦρμο! κάτω, Τσοῦρμο!» Ὁ Τσοῦρμος ὑπήκουεν, ἀλλὰ μετὰ δυσκολίας, κ' ἐξέφραζε τὴν λύπην του διὰ παρατεταμένων γαυγισμῶν. Ἤρχισε νὰ κυκλοφορῇ τὸ ποτήριον τῆς ρακῆς, καὶ οἱ ναυπηγοὶ ὅλοι καὶ οἱ περιπατηταὶ ἔλεγαν τὰς συνήθεις εὐχάς: «Καλορρίζικο! μάλαμα τὸ καρφί τ', καπετάνιο! Καλὸ πλέψιμο!» Τὴν τελευταίαν λέξιν οἱ πλεῖστοι ἐπρόφεραν, κατὰ παραφθοράν, *πλέξιμο*. Καὶ εἷς περίεργος ἄνθρωπος μὲ χονδρὸν ἄσχημον πρόσωπον, μὲ παχύτατον μύστακα ἐπικαθήμενον ὡς στοιβιὰ ἐπὶ τῶν μήλων τῶν παρειῶν του, ἕως τοὺς ὀφθαλμούς, ἡμιναύτης καὶ ἡμιεργάτης καὶ ἡμιεκφορτωτὴς (οὗτος ἦτο ὁ Ἀλέξανδρος Χάραυλος, ὁ ἴδιος ὅστις πηδαλιουχῶν ποτὲ ἐν μακρῷ ταξιδίῳ, κατὰ τὴν Μαύρην Θάλασσαν, ἐπὶ μεγάλου πλοίου, τὴν νύκτα, ἠρωτήθη ὑπὸ τοῦ πλοιάρχου, περιπατοῦντος κατὰ μῆκος τοῦ καταστρώματος ἀπὸ τὴν πρύμνην ἕως τὴν πρῶραν: «Τί ἔχεις, βρὲ Ἀλέξανδρε, κι ἀναστενάζεις;» κ' ἐκεῖνος ἀπήντησε: «Συλλογίζομαι, καπετάνιε, πῶς θὰ τὰ πληρώσουμε, τόσα ἑκατομμύρια ποὺ χρωστάει τὸ

* * *

Meanwhile the sun had hidden behind the peak of the high rocky mountain, and the driller's shadow was expunged from the surface of the water and the sand of the beach. The builders, along with the many evening strollers who had come to offer visual support to the workers in their toil and occasionally to delay them with their untimely questions, stepped over the beams, ribs and unhewn timbers strewn all over the boatyard, and gathered in a confused swarm around the captain's hut, which was full of cleats and other bits of wood, baskets of tools, clothes and bed-covers, to drink *tsipouro** poured from a great demijohn, everyone using the same glass. The huge ship's dog, tied by a sturdy chain outside the hut behind the stern of the great ship, let out the occasional muffled threatening growl, as if he alone could distinguish the buzz of the drones from the buzz of the workers, and seemed ready to pounce if only someone would untie him. But Captain Yorgakis, who looked quite cultivated, with his long, hooked, fair mustachios, his sunburned complexion and his short stature, restrained the dog's impetuousness with curt shouts of, 'Back, Tsourmos! Down, Tsourmos!' Tsourmos reluctantly obeyed, expressing his frustration with prolonged barking. The spirit-glass began circulating, and all the builders and strollers proposed the customary toasts: 'Good luck! May her nails be golden, Captain! Good sailing!' A certain curious fellow with coarse, ugly features and a thick moustache planted like a thorny burnet between his cheeks and reaching right up to his eyes, half-sailor, half-workman and half-stevedore — this was Alexandros Charavlos, the same man who, one night, while steering a large ship during a long voyage in the Black Sea, when asked by the captain as he paced up and down the deck between stern and bows, 'What's the matter with you, Alexandros? Why are you sighing?', replied, 'Captain, I'm wondering how we're going to pay back all those millions the country owes!' — this Alexandros Charavlos, who was more than a little simple and had been hired

Ἔθνος!»)· οὗτος λοιπὸν ὁ Ἀλέξανδρος Χάραυλος, ὀλίγον πέραν τοῦ δέοντος ἀφελής, προσληφθεὶς ἀπὸ τῆς προτεραίας διὰ νὰ ὑπηρετῇ εἰς τὴν ναυπήγησιν τοῦ σκάφους, ὅταν ἦλθεν ἡ σειρά του διὰ νὰ πίῃ καὶ νὰ χαιρετίσῃ, ἐπρόφερεν ἐξ ὑπερβαλλούσης ἀδεξιότητος ὡς ἑξῆς τὴν ἀνωτέρω σημειωθεῖσαν λέξιν: «Καλὸ *μπλέξιμο*, καπετάνιο!» Οἱ ἄλλοι ἐκάγχασαν· ὁ ξανθομούστακος πλοίαρχος συνωφρυώθη, ὁ Τσοῦρμος ἠγέρθη ἐπὶ τῶν ὀπισθίων ποδῶν καὶ ἀφῆκε φοβερὰν ὑλακήν! Ὁ ἀδελφὸς τοῦ πλοιάρχου, ὁ Δημήτρης ὁ Τσιμπίδας, ἤγειρε τὴν χεῖρα ν' ἁρπάσῃ ἀπὸ τὸν σβέρκον τὸν Ἀλέξανδρον τὸν Χάραυλον καὶ νὰ τοῦ καταφέρῃ ὀλίγους κονδύλους. Ὁ καπετὰν Γιωργάκης τὸν ἐμπόδισεν, ἂν καὶ τοῦ ἐκόστισε πολύ. Διότι ὅλοι οἱ ναυτικοί, καὶ οἱ πλέον μορφωμένοι σχετικῶς, δὲν εἶναι ἀπηλλαγμένοι δεισιδαιμονιῶν καὶ προλήψεων. Πῶς νὰ μὴν εἶναί τις δεισιδαίμων ὅταν «πολεμῇ μὲ τὸ μεγαλύτερον θηρίον», ὅταν παλαίῃ μὲ τὸ ἄγνωστον, καὶ δὲν ἠξεύρῃ ἂν αὔριον θὰ ἐπιπλέῃ ἢ θὰ ποντισθῇ, ἂν θὰ εἶναι εἰς τὴν ἐπιφάνειαν ἢ εἰς τὸν πυθμένα; Ὁ πλοίαρχος ἠρκέσθη μόνον νὰ εἴπῃ ὀργίλως:

— Δάκω τή γλῶσσα σ', βρὲ στραβο-Χάραυλε... νὰ μὴν ἁρπάξω τή σαλαμάστρα, τώρα...

Καὶ μετὰ δυσκολίας πολλῆς ἐμπόδισε τὸν ἀδελφόν του νὰ μὴ τὸν αἰκίσῃ.

* * *

Ἐκεῖ, ὄπισθεν τῶν θάμνων τοῦ φράκτου, ἐν μέσῳ τῶν χωραφίων, — τῶν — ἀμπέλων καὶ τοῦ αἰγιαλοῦ, ὅπου ὄχι σπανίως ἡ μὲν θάλασσα ἐπάτει καὶ ἀφωμοίου τὸ ἥμισυ κήπου ἢ ἀγροῦ μὲ συκᾶς, μηλέας καὶ ἀπιδέας, οἱ δὲ διαβάται ἔκαμναν δρόμον τὸ ἄλλο ἥμισυ τοῦ αὐτοῦ κήπου ἢ ἀγροῦ (καὶ οἱ εὐτυχεῖς ἰδιοκτῆται εἰς ποῖον νὰ προσκλαυθῶσιν;) ἤκουες πολλάκις τὴν ἑσπέραν περὶ τὸ λυκόφως, ἐνῷ οἱ ναυπηγοὶ φορτωμένοι τὰ ζεμπίλια μὲ τὰ σιδερικά των ἐπέστρεφαν εἰς τὴν πολίχνην, ἤκουες, μεταξὺ δύο ἢ τριῶν μαραγκῶν, μετρούντων τὰς ἡμέρας ἕωσοῦ ἔλθῃ ἡ πρώτη Κυριακή, κατόπιν τῆς ὁποίας εἴποντο κατὰ σειρὰν τρεῖς ἢ τέσσαρες ἑορταί (τῶν Κορυφαίων Ἀποστόλων, τῶν Δώδεκα, τῶν Ἁγίων Ἀναργύρων καὶ τῆς Ἁγίας Ἐσθῆτος), καὶ ἀναλογιζομένων μετὰ προαπολαύσεως μελλούσης μακαριότητος ὅτι θὰ ἔπλεον ὅσον οὔπω ἀντικρύ, εἰς τὴν ἀνατολικὴν νῆσον, τὴν κρατοῦσαν δέσμια πανταχόσε τῆς γῆς ὅλα τὰ

the previous day to help with the building of the ship, when his turn came to drink to its good fortune, by a clumsy slip of the tongue, uttered the last toast as 'Good failing, Captain!' The others chortled, but the fair-moustached captain frowned, while Tsourmos reared up on his hind legs and let out a fearsome bark. The captain's brother, Dimitris Tsimbidas, raised his hand to seize Alexandros Charavlos by the scruff of his neck and give him a few hefty cuffs. However, Captain Yorgakis prevented him, despite the fact that he had to make an effort to restrain himself too, since no sailor, even those relatively educated, is free of superstitious fears. How can one not be superstitious when he is struggling with that greatest of monsters, wrestling with the unknown, never certain whether tomorrow he will be sailing or sinking? The captain confined himself to shouting angrily:

'Hold your tongue, Charavlos, you idiot, or I'll grab the hawser and...'

It was with great difficulty that he prevented his brother from thrashing him.

* * *

There, behind the bushy hedgerow, between the fields, the vineyards and the shore, where not infrequently the sea would trespass in an attempt to appropriate half a garden or an orchard of figs, apples and pears, while passers-by made the other half of the same garden or orchard into a road (and who could the happy owners complain to?), in the evening, around dusk, as the ship-builders, loaded with their baskets of tools, were returning to the little town, you would often hear a conversation between two or three carpenters counting the days until the first Sunday that would be followed by three or four feast days in succession (those of the Apostles Peter and Paul, the Twelve Apostles, Sts Cosmas and Damian, and the Deposition of the Holy Robe of the Virgin Mary)* and joyfully anticipating the pleasure with which they would shortly sail across, crammed into two heavy cargo boats, the work of their own hands, for a four-day holiday on the eastern island over yonder,* which kept all

τέκνα της μὲ ἀόρατον συμπαθὲς νῆμα πόθου καὶ νοσταλγίας, θὰ ἔπλεον ὅλοι στοιβαζόμενοι εἰς δύο μεγάλας ὁλκάδας, ἔργα τῶν χειρῶν των, ὅπως ἐπὶ τετραήμερον ἑορτάσωσιν· ἤκουες, λέγω, διάλογον οἷος ὁ ἑξῆς:

—Νά, κοντεύουμε τώρα, Νταντή...

—Ἀργοῦμε ἀκόμα, Μπεφάνη...

—Τί λές, βρὲ Νταντή;... Δευτέρα πέρασε, Τρίτ' Τετράδ' μιά, Πέφτ' Παρασκευὴ δυό, Σάββατο, πρῶτα ὁ Θεός, εἴμαστε πέρα.

Καὶ *οὕτως ὁδὸς μακρὰ βραχεῖα γίγνεται*, ὄχι κατὰ τὸν Σοφοκλέα.

Ἀλλὰ δὲν ἦτο πάντοτε ἑσπέρα ὅταν ἔβαινες πρὸς τὴν ἀμμώδη ἐκείνην παραλίαν μὲ τ' ἀβαθῆ ὕδατα, καὶ δὲν ἔβλεπες πάντοτε ὁμάδας ἀνθρώπων ἐπιστρεφόντων ἐκ τοῦ ναυπηγείου, οὐδὲ πτωχῶν γυναικῶν φορτωμένων σάκκους πλήρεις πελεκουδίων ἐπὶ τῶν ἰσχνῶν ὤμων των. Ἦτο πρωία, καὶ δὲν εἶχε παρέλθει ὁ χειμών, καὶ δὲν εἶχαν σκαρώσει ἀκόμη τὰ μεγάλα σκάφη. Εἰς τὸ ναυπηγεῖον μία μόνον βρατσέρα καὶ δύο βάρκαι μικραὶ ὑπῆρχαν σκαρωμέναι. Δὲν εἰργάζοντο ἐκεῖ εἰμὴ ὁ μαστρο-Γιωργός, Θεὸς σχωρέσ' τον, ὁ Βαγγελάκης, μὲ τὴν κοκκίνην σκούφιαν του, ἥτις δὲν ἦτο οὔτε φέσι οὔτε κοῦκος οὔτε καπέλο, ἀλλὰ μετεῖχεν ἀπὸ ὅλα αὐτά, μὲ τοὺς πισσωμένους ἀμπάδες του καὶ μὲ τὴν πολύχρουν ἀπὸ τὰ ἐμβαλώματα καμιζόλαν του, καὶ ὁ Γιάννης τῆς Παναγιοῦς, μὲ τὸ ὑψηλὸν καὶ ὀρθὸν φέσι του, μὲ τὴν μακρὰν καὶ πολύπτυχον βράκαν του, μὲ τὴν ἄσπρην φανέλαν καὶ μὲ τὴν μεγάλην ζεμπίλαν του. Ὁ ἥλιος μόλις εἶχεν ἀνατείλει, διαλύων τοὺς ἀνερχομένους ἀπὸ τὴν θάλασσαν πρὸς τὴν πρασινίζουσαν ἀκτὴν λευκοὺς ἀτμούς, τὰ ὕδατα ἦσαν ῥηχὰ ἀπὸ τὸν ἀσθενῆ ἄνεμον ὅστις ἐφύσα. Ἐφαίνετο τὴν πρωίαν ἐκείνην ὅτι καὶ αὐτὸς ὁ Βορρᾶς εὑρέθη εἰς διάθεσιν φιλοπαίγμονα, θωπεύων μαλακὰ τὴν θάλασσαν. Καὶ ἡ ψυχρὰ ῥιπὴ δὲν ἦτο δυσάρεστος εἰς τὸν μικρὸν κτηματίαν τὸν ἐπιβαίνοντα τοῦ ὄνου καὶ ἀπερχόμενον εἰς τὸν ἀγρόν του, οὐδὲ εἰς τὸν ζευγηλάτην, τὸν διὰ τῆς φωνῆς ἀποτείνοντα τὰ κελεύσματα εἰς τοὺς βόες του: «Ὤ! Μελίσσ', ὄξου Μαυρομμάτ'!» καὶ διὰ τοῦ βλέμματος θωπεύοντα τὴν μεγάλην χύτραν μὲ τὰ καλομαγειρευμένα μὲ ἱκανὸν εὐῶδες ἔλαιον φασόλια, καὶ μὲ ἄφθονον κοκκίνην πιπεριάν, τὴν ὁποίαν, μὲ τὸ ἐξησκημένον βλέμμα του, εἶχεν ἀνακαλύψει ἤδη ἐρχομένην ὄπισθεν τῶν θάμνων, ὁλονὲν καὶ πλησιάζουσαν σκεπασμένην καλὰ διὰ νὰ μὴν κρυώσῃ τὸ φαγητόν, ἐπιστέφουσαν τὸν μέγαν κόφινον, ἐπὶ τῶν ὤμων τῆς φιλοτίμου οἰκοκυρᾶς,

her children, wherever in the world they might be, tied to her with an invisible emotional thread of longing and nostalgia; you would often hear, I say, a conversation such as the following:

'There, we're getting close, Dadis.'

'We've still got a long way to go, Befanis.'

'What do you mean, Dadis? Monday's gone, Tuesday, Wednesday, that's one, Thursday, Friday, that's two, Saturday, God willing, we're there.'

And 'thus does a long road become short', but not according to Sophocles.*

But it wasn't always evening when you walked to that sandy beach with its shallow waters, and you didn't always see groups of men returning from the boatyard, nor groups of poor women, their thin shoulders laden with sacks of wood-chips. It was morning, and the winter had not passed, and the big ships had not yet been put on the stocks. In the boatyard just one lugger and two small dinghies were under construction. The only people working there were master shipbuilder Yorgos Vangelakis, God rest his soul, with his red cap, which was neither a fez nor a beret nor a brimmed hat, but partook of all of these, with his tar-lined canvas shoes and his smock many-coloured from all its patches, and Panayou's son Yannis, with his tall, upright cap, his long pleated breeches, his white vest and his big basket. The sun had only just risen, dissipating the white mist that rose from the sea towards the verdant shore, and the water rippled in the light breeze. That morning even the north wind seemed to find itself in a playful mood, softly caressing the sea. The nip in the air was not displeasing to the farmer riding his donkey out to his field, nor to the ploughman shouting orders to his oxen: 'Whoa, Honey! Gee-up, Blackeye!', and caressing with his gaze the large saucepan of beans, well cooked in abundant fragrant olive oil and with plenty of red pepper, which his trained eye had espied coming along behind the hedge, gradually approaching, well covered so that the food would not get cold, crowning the large basket on the shoulders of the dutiful housewife, almost sailing

But you, friend, took no notice of these trivial things, but envied far more the little ten-year-old boys hitching their trousers up to their thighs... [p. 39]

σχεδὸν ἀρμενίζουσαν ὡς βάρκαν, χωρὶς νὰ φαίνωνται οὔτε αἱ χεῖρες αἱ ὑποβαστάζουσαι οὔτε οἱ πόδες οἱ βηματίζοντες. Ὀλίγαι στιγμαὶ θὰ παρήρχοντο ἀκόμη, καὶ ὁ μὲν Μελίσσης καὶ ὁ Μαυρομμάτης, ἀπολυόμενοι πρὸς ὥραν τοῦ ζυγοῦ, θὰ ἔβοσκον μακαρίως παρὰ τὰς χονδρὰς καὶ ὀζώδεις ῥίζας τῶν ἐλαιῶν, ὁ δὲ ζευγηλάτης καὶ ὁ βοηθός του, θὰ παρεκάθιζον ἐπιφθόνως ὑπὸ τὸ εὐλογημένον φύλλωμα, καὶ θὰ ἐπειρῶντο ἐγγύτερον τῆς χύτρας.

Ἀλλὰ σύ, φίλε, δὲν προσεῖχες τότε εἰς τὰ τετριμμένα αὐτά, ἀλλ' ἐφθόνεις μᾶλλον τοὺς μικροὺς δεκαετεῖς παῖδας, τοὺς ἀνασηκώνοντας τὴν περισκελίδα ὡς τὸν μηρόν, φέροντας τὰ πέδιλα εἰς τὸ θυλάκιον καὶ

...as he dashed from reed-bed to reed-bed, looking at the rushes and sighing because he had not fished as many perch and red mullet as there were rushes... [p. 43]

like a boat, although he could not see the hands that steadied it or the feet that walked beneath it. A few more moments would go by, and Honey and Blackeye, temporarily released from the yoke, would graze blissfully by the thick, gnarled roots of the olives, while the ploughman and his boy would sit down enviably under the blessed foliage as close as possible to the saucepan.

But you, friend, took no notice of these trivial things, but envied far more the little ten-year-old boys hitching their trousers up to their thighs, stuffing their shoes into their pockets and

θαλασσώνοντας ὑπὲρ τὸ γόνυ εἰς τὸ κῦμα. Ἔβλεπες ἔξαφνα ἕνα τούτων νὰ κύπτῃ νὰ συλλαμβάνῃ μὲ τὴν παλάμην μικρὸν ὀκταπόδιον, νὰ τὸ δαγκάνῃ εἰς τὸν λαιμόν, ν' ἀγωνίζεται ν' ἀποσπάσῃ ἀπὸ τὸν καρπὸν τῆς χειρός του τοὺς μυζητῆρας, νὰ τρέχῃ εἰς τὴν ἄμμον καὶ νὰ τὸ κοπανίζῃ γενναίως εἰς τὸν πρῶτον λίθον τὸν ὁποῖον θὰ εὕρισκε, λείψανον παρασυρθέντος ἀπὸ τὰ κύματα ξηρολιθίνου περιβόλου κήπου ἢ ἐρείπιον πάλαι ποτὲ ὑπαρξάσης προκυμαίας. Καὶ ἡ μήτηρ σου ἡ φιλότεκνος ὄχι μόνον δὲν σοῦ ἐπέτρεπε νὰ τρέχῃς, ὅπως ἄλλοι, ἀνυπόδητος καὶ σύ, ἀλλ' ἀπῄτει νὰ φορῇς καὶ κάλτσες. Ὁποῖα δεσμὰ παιδαγωγικῆς δουλοσύνης! Εὐτυχῶς εἶχες πλησίον σου τὸν φίλον σου, τὸν Χριστοδουλήν, ὅστις, ὁμῆλιξ μὲ σέ, ἦτο εὐτυχέστερος κατὰ τοῦτο, ὅτι ἦτο πάντοτε ξυπόλυτος, καὶ οὐδ' ἐφόρει ποτὲ κάλτσες. Φιλότιμον παιδίον! Ἔτρεχε δι' ὅλης τῆς ἡμέρας ἀπὸ γιαλὸν εἰς γιαλόν, ἔβγαζε γρινιάτσες, πορφύρες καὶ πεταλίδες διὰ δύο, καβούρια διὰ τρεῖς, ὀκταπόδια διὰ τέσσαρες. Καὶ μέρος μὲν αὐτῶν ἔκαμνε δολώματα, διὰ νὰ ψαρεύῃ μὲ τὴν καλαμιὰν ἀπὸ τὸ δειλινὸν ἕως τὸ βράδυ, μέρος δὲ ἐμοιράζετο φιλαδέλφως μὲ σέ. Τὴν πρωίαν ἐκείνην ὀλίγον πρὶν φθάσητε εἰς τὸν μῦλον τοῦ Μπαρμπαπαναγιώτη, ὅστις ἵσταται ὡς φρουρὸς παρὰ τὸ δυτικὸν στόμιον τῆς λίμνης, ἐκεῖ ὅπου ἦτο οὐδέτερον ἔδαφος μεταξὺ θαλάσσης καὶ ξηρᾶς, ὁ φίλος σου ὁ Χριστοδουλής, ἐπειδὴ εἰς τὸ μέρος τοῦτο τὰ ὕδατα ἐβαθύνοντο ὀλίγον τι ἀποτόμως, δὲν εὑρίσκετο πολὺ μακρὰν εἰς τὸ κῦμα, καὶ ἅμα εἶδεν ὅτι ἡ Πολύμνια πλησιάσασα ἤρχισε νὰ σοῦ ὁμιλῇ, ἔσπευσε νὰ ἀποβῇ εἰς τὴν ξηρὰν διὰ ν' ἀκούσῃ τί σοῦ ἔλεγε.

Ὁποῖον λεπτοφυὲς σῶμα ἐσκέπαζεν ἡ λειομέταξος ὀρφνὴ ἐσθής! Πῶς διεγράφετο ἁρμονικῶς ἡ μορφή της μὲ χνοώδη πάλλευκον χρῶτα καὶ τὰ ἐρυθρὰ μῆλα τῶν παρειῶν, μὲ τὸν μελίχρυσον λαιμὸν καὶ μὲ τὸ ἐλαφρῶς κολπούμενον στῆθός της! Πόσον ἁβραὶ ἦσαν αἱ χεῖρες, καὶ πόσον μελωδικὴ ἔπαλλεν εἰς τὸ οὖς σου ἡ θεσπεσία φωνή της! Ἡ ξανθοπλόκαμος κόμη ἀτημέλητος ὀλίγον, ὡς νὰ ἐβιάσθη νὰ καλλωπισθῇ διὰ νὰ ἐξέλθῃ καὶ ἀπολαύσῃ τὴν θαλασσίαν αὔραν καὶ τὸν τερπνὸν τῆς ἀμμουδιᾶς περίπατον, ἀερίζετο ἀπὸ τὴν πνοὴν τοῦ Βορρᾶ, καὶ τὸ ὄμμα της, μὲ τὰ μακρὰ ματόκλαδα ὡς πτεροφόρος ὀιστός, σ' ἐσαΐτευε γλυκὰ εἰς τὴν καρδίαν. Ἐνθυμεῖσαι! Ὁποῖον αἴσθημα ἐδοκίμασες τότε, καὶ πῶς, δεκατετραετὴς μόλις, ἠρωτεύθης

wading knee-deep into the water. You would suddenly see one of them bending down to catch a small octopus in his hand, bite it behind the head, struggle to detach the suckers from his wrist, run to the sand and give it a generous beating on the first large stone he found, a remnant of an orchard's dry-stone wall washed away by the waves, or of a now ruined jetty. Your loving mother not only forbade you to run barefoot like other children, but demanded that you wear socks as well. What bonds of pedagogical servitude! Fortunately you had your friend Christodoulis near you, who, while he was the same age as you, was more fortunate in that he was always barefoot and never wore socks. What an obliging child! All day he would run from beach to beach, gathering enough rock snails, limpets and other shellfish for two, enough crabs for three, and enough octopuses for four. One portion of these he used as bait when he went fishing with his rod from early evening till nightfall, while another he shared fraternally with you. That morning, shortly before you both arrived at old *Barba*-Panayotis's mill, which stood guard over the neutral territory between sea and land by the western mouth of the lagoon, your friend Christodoulis wasn't very far out, since at that point the sea bottom shelved down rather steeply, and as soon as he saw that Polymnia had approached you and started talking to you, he hastened to come out of the water to listen to what she was saying.

What a slenderly built figure was concealed by that dark dress woven from linen and silk, how harmoniously delineated was her face, with her downy white complexion and her red cheeks, her honey-gold neck and her slightly swelling bosom! How soft were those hands, how melodiously the sound of her divine voice vibrated in your ears! Her blond plaited hair, slightly unkempt as though she had hurried her toilet so as to get out and enjoy the delights of a walk along the beach in the sea-breeze, was blown by the north wind's breath, and her eyes, like feathered arrows with their long lashes, shot sweetly piercing glances into your heart. Do you remember what you felt at that moment, and how,

ἤδη; Ἡ Πολύμνια σοῦ ὡμίλησεν! Ἡ Πολύμνια σ' ἐκάλει ὀνομαστί! Ὁποία παιδικὴ μέθη, εὐκόλως παραχθεῖσα διὰ μικρᾶς δόσεως ρευστοῦ! Ἐφαίνετο ὅτι *δὲν ἐσήκωνες περισσότερον*. Καὶ ὅμως, τὸ πρᾶγμα ἦτο ἁπλούστατον. Ὁ ἀδελφός της, δωδεκαέτης, ἐκεῖνος ἤξευρε τ' ὄνομά σου καὶ εἶπε τίς εἶσαι εἰς τὴν Πολύμνιαν. Καὶ αὕτη δὲν ἐνόμισεν ὅτι θὰ ἐσαγίτευε τὴν καρδίαν σου, ἂν σοῦ ἀπέτεινε τὸν λόγον, ἀφοῦ μάλιστα ἤθελε νὰ σοῦ ζητήσῃ ἐκδούλευσιν. Ἐν τούτοις ὁ Χριστοδουλῆς ἔτρεξε πλησίον σου, καταβιβάσας ἐν σπουδῇ τὴν περισκελίδα του, ὡς διὰ νὰ μοιρασθῇ τὸ βάρος τῆς εὐτυχίας.

Ἡ μελῳδικὴ φωνὴ τῆς Πολυμνίας εἶπε:

— Ξέρεις, ποῦ εἶναι ἴτσια; Μπορεῖς νὰ μοῦ κόψῃς τίποτε ἴτσια;

Σὺ ἔμενες κεχηνώς.

Ἀλλ' εὐτυχῶς ὁ Χριστοδουλῆς εἶχε φθάσει ἤδη.

— Μπράβο! μπράβο!... κυρία Πολύμνια! Ἐγὼ τὰ ξέρω ποῦ εἶναι τὰ ἴτσια... τώρα νὰ πᾶμε νὰ κόψουμε...

— Θὰ μὲ ὑποχρεώσετε πολύ, ἐπανέλαβε καὶ πρὸς τοὺς δύο ἡ Πολύμνια.

Καὶ ὁ Χριστοδουλῆς ἔτρεξεν ἐλαφρόπους, μὲ τὸ ἓν μπουδονάρι του ἀνασηκωμένον ἀκόμη ἕως τὸ γόνυ, μὲ τὸ ἄλλο καταβιβασμένον εἰς τὸν ἀστράγαλον, ξυπόλυτος, μὲ τὰ πόδια *παπουδιασμένα*, μαῦρα, ψημένα ἀπὸ τὴν ἅλμην τοῦ κύματος. Ἔτρεξες καὶ σὺ κατόπιν του ὀκνός, ἀσθμαίνων, ἀλλ' ἕως νὰ φθάσῃς εἰς τὴν ὄχθην τῆς λίμνης, πατῶν ἐπὶ τοῦ ὀλισθηροῦ βάλτου, γλιστρῶν, ἀνάμεσα εἰς τὲς ἁρμυρήθρες καὶ εἰς τὲς βουρλιές, ὁ Χριστοδουλῆς εἶχε κόψει ἤδη ὁλόκληρον δεσμίδα ἐκ τῶν πρωίμων εὐωδῶν καὶ μεθυστικῶν ἀνθέων, τὰ ὁποῖα ἐζήτει ἡ Πολύμνια, τρέχων ἀπὸ συστάδα χόρτου εἰς συστάδα, αἵτινες ἐσκίαζον φιλαδέλφως τὰ πτωχὰ ὡραῖα ἄνθη, τὰ τόσον τρυφερὰ καὶ ἀσθενῆ, μὲ τὰ λευκὰ πέταλα καὶ τὸν ὠχρὸν ὕπερον, τὰ ὁποῖα ἐφαίνοντο ὡς νὰ παραπονοῦνται διατί νὰ φύωνται εἰς τὸ χῶμα καὶ νὰ εἶναι τόσον χαμαιπετῆ· ὁ Χριστοδουλῆς τὰ ἔκοπτεν ἀσπλάγχνως, ἀνὰ δύο καὶ τρία, μεμειγμένα μὲ χόρτα, καὶ τὰ ἐστοίβαζεν ἐπὶ τῆς ὠλένης τῆς χειρός του, μεταβαίνων ἀπὸ βουρλιὰν εἰς βουρλιάν, βλέπων τὰ βοῦρλα καὶ ἀναστενάζων, διατί νὰ μὴν ἔχῃ ἁλιεύσει μὲ τὰς χεῖράς του τόσες πέρκες, καὶ τριγλία, ὅσα βοῦρλα ἔβλεπε, καὶ διατί νὰ μὴ δύναται νὰ χρησιμοποιήσῃ ταῦτα ὅπως ὁρμαθιάσῃ ἐκεῖνα.

scarcely fourteen years old, you had already fallen in love? Polymnia had spoken to you! Polymnia was calling you by name! What childish intoxication, effortlessly induced by such a small draught! You felt as though you couldn't take any more. And yet there was a simple explanation. Her twelve-year-old brother knew your name and had told Polymnia who you were. As for her, it hadn't occurred to her that she would be shooting arrows into your heart if she addressed you, since all she wanted was to ask you a favour. Meanwhile Christodoulis was running up to you, hurriedly rolling down his trousers, as if to share the burden of your happiness.

Polymnia's melodious voice said:

'Do you know where there the narcissus grows? Could you pick me some?'

You remained open-mouthed. But fortunately Christodoulis had arrived.

'Why certainly, Miss Polymnia, I know where they are. We'll go and pick some now.'

'I shall be much obliged to you,' said Polymnia to us both.

Christodoulis ran off, light-footed, one trouser-leg still rolled up to the knee and the other down to his ankle, without shoes, the skin of his feet tanned by the brine and puckered from long immersion in the water. You ran after him, sluggish and panting, but, by the time you reached the shore of the lagoon, stepping into the slippery mud, sliding amongst the glasswort and the bulrushes, Christodoulis had already picked a whole bunch of those early, intoxicatingly fragrant flowers that Polymnia had asked for, running between the clumps of grass that lovingly shaded those humble but beautiful blooms, so tender and delicate, with their white petals and their yellow trumpets, which seemed to regret that they grew on the earth and were so lowly. Christodoulis picked them pitilessly, in twos and threes, mixed with grass, and bundled them in the crook of his arm as he dashed from reed-bed to reed-bed, looking at the rushes and sighing because he had not fished as many perch and red mullet as there were rushes, and had not used the latter to string the former in bunches.

Μέχρις οὗ κατορθώσῃς καὶ σὺ νὰ εὕρῃς ὀλίγα ἴτσια νὰ κόψῃς, ὁ Χριστοδουλῆς εἶχε καταρτίσει ἤδη ὁλόκληρον ἀγκαλίδα, κ' ἐπέστρεφε τρέχων πρὸς τὸν ἀνεμόμυλον, ἐκεῖ ὅπου ἵστατο περιμένουσα μετὰ τοῦ ἀδελφοῦ της ἡ Πολύμνια. Ἐν τούτοις ἐπρόφθασες καὶ σὺ καὶ τῆς ἔφερες μικράν, ὅση ἠδύνατο νὰ συνθλιβῇ μεταξὺ ἀντίχειρος καὶ λιχανοῦ, δεσμίδα, ἀλλὰ τὸ *εὐχαριστῶ* τὸ πρὸς σὲ ἦτο, ὡς εἰκός, χλιαρώτερον ἀπὸ τὸ *εὐχαριστῶ* τὸ πρὸς τὸν φίλον σου. Καὶ οὐχ ἧττον ἔμεινες εὐχαριστημένος, ὀλιγαρκὴς καὶ κυριευόμενος ὑπὸ αὐταρέσκου νάρκης, ὁμωνύμου μὲ τὸ τρυφερὸν ἐκεῖνο ἄνθος, τὸ ὁποῖον ἐζήτει μὲν ἀπὸ σέ, ἔλαβε δὲ ἀπὸ τὸν φίλον σου ἡ Πολύμνια.

* * *

Ἔκτοτε ὁ Χριστοδουλῆς ἠραίωσε κατ' ἀρχάς, εἶτα ὁριστικῶς ἔπαυσε, τὸ μερίδιον, τὸ ὁποῖον σοῦ ἔδιδε τέως ἀπὸ τὰ κογχύλια, ἀπὸ τὰ καβούρια καὶ ἀπὸ τοὺς γωβιούς, σὺ δὲ ἤργησες πολὺ νὰ μάθῃς ὅτι τὰ ἔδιδεν εἰς τὸν Νῖκον, τὸν ἀδελφὸν τῆς Πολυμνίας. Εἰς μάτην τὸν συνώδευες, ὡς πάντοτε, βαδίζων ἐπὶ τῆς ἄμμου, θαλασσώνοντα ἕως τὸν μηρόν, καὶ ἀπὸ καιροῦ εἰς καιρὸν τοῦ ἐφώναζες:

— Κ'στοδουλή, βρέ! δὲν ἔβγαλες ἀκόμη κανένα χταπόδι;

Ἐκεῖνος τὰ χταπόδια καὶ τὰ καβουράκια τὰ ἔβαζεν εἰς τὸν φουσκωμένον καὶ βρεγμένον κόλπον τοῦ ὑποκαμίσου του, ἔχων τρόπον νὰ τὰ ψοφᾷ μὲ δαγκωματιὲς καὶ μὲ ἀκρωτηριασμούς, καὶ σοῦ ἔδειχνε μόνον τὲς γρινιάτσες, λέγων ὅτι θὰ ὑπάγῃ ὕστερ' ἀπὸ τὸ μεσημέρι, νὰ ψαρέψῃ μὲ τὴν καλαμιά. Καὶ ὅταν, περὶ τὴν δείλην, τὸν παρεμόνευες, παρὰ τὴν ἀγοράν, ἐπὶ τῆς ἀποβάθρας, κ' ἔβλεπες ἰδίοις ὄμμασι νὰ σπαρταρίζῃ κανεὶς γωβιὸς εἰς τὸ ἄκρον τοῦ ἀγκίστρου του, καὶ τότε σ' ἐγέλα λέγων ὅτι θὰ κάμῃ τὸν γωβιὸν δόλωμα διὰ νὰ βγάλῃ μεγάλα ψάρια. Οὕτω χάνεται ἡ φιλία!

Πολλαὶ πρωῖαι διέρρευσαν κατόπιν τῆς πρωΐας ἐκείνης τοῦ φθίνοντος Φεβρουαρίου. Ἐπέρασεν ὁλόκληρος ὁ Μάρτιος, ἦλθε καὶ τὸ Πάσχα, παρῆλθε καὶ ὁ Ἀπρίλιος, καὶ ἡ Πολύμνια δὲν ἐξῆλθε πλέον εἰς περίπατον πρὸς τὴν παραθαλασσίαν τοῦ ναυπηγείου. Εἰς μάτην ἔτρεχες τακτικὰ κάθε πρωΐαν κ' ἑσπέραν εἰς τὴν ἀμμουδιὰν ἐκείνην. Ἡ Πολύμνια καθὼς ἀργὰ ἔμαθες εἶχεν ἀρρωστήσει ἀρχομένου τοῦ ἔαρος, κατὰ τὴν συμβουλὴν δὲ τῶν ἰατρῶν εἶχε κάμει, περὶ τὸν Μάιον,

By the time you had managed to find a few narcissi to pick, Christodoulis had already gathered a whole sheaf and was running back towards the windmill where Polymnia stood waiting with her brother. You arrived at the same time, bringing her a little bunch, small enough to be held between forefinger and thumb, and her 'thank you' to you was, as expected, more lukewarm than her 'thank you' to your friend. But you were nonetheless gratified, satisfied with little, overcome by a complacent torpor that resembled the tender flower that Polymnia had sought from you but had received from your friend.

* * *

From then on Christodoulis began to decrease, and then discontinued, the share that he had formerly given you of his shellfish, crabs and gobies, and you soon found out that he was giving them to Polymnia's brother Nikos. In vain did you accompany him, as always, walking along the road as he waded in up to his thighs, and occasionally shouting to him:

'Hey, Christodoulis! Haven't you caught an octopus yet?'

He would put the crabs and octopuses in the bulge of his wet shirt, knowing the knack of killing them with bites and amputations, and showed you only the limpets, saying that he would go fishing in the afternoon with his rod. And when in the evening you looked out for him on the quayside near the market and you actually saw a goby wriggling on the end of his hook, he would pretend that he was going to use it for bait to catch some bigger fish. That's how friends are lost!

Many mornings slipped by after that morning in late February. The whole of March went by, then Easter came, and April, and Polymnia never went out for a walk again along the seashore to the boatyard. In vain did you run to the beach regularly every morning and evening. You later learned that Polymnia had fallen ill at the beginning of spring, and around May, on the advice of the doctors, she had gone on a journey for a change of air with her aunt, who received a state pension

ταξίδιον μετὰ τῆς θείας της, τῆς συνταξιούχου, χήρας ἀντιπλοιάρχου τοῦ Β. στόλου, διὰ ν' ἀλλάξῃ τὸν ἀέρα. Τρία μεγάλα σκάφη εἶχαν σκαρωθῆ ἀπὸ τῶν πρώτων ἡμερῶν τοῦ Μαρτίου, καὶ σὺ δὲν ἔπαυες νὰ τρέχῃς καθ' ἑκάστην ἕως τὸ ναυπηγεῖον, σταματῶν ἐπὶ ὥρας πολλάκις παρὰ τὸν ἀνεμόμυλον, καθεζόμενος ἐπὶ τῶν κάτω κειμένων καταρτίων πάλαι ποτὲ ὑπαρξάσης γολέτας, ἀναπολῶν ὅτι εἰς τὸ μέρος ἐκεῖνο ἐστάθη πρὸ μηνῶν ἡ Πολύμνια, ὅταν σοῦ ἐζήτησε νὰ δρέψῃς πρὸς χάριν της ἴτσια· ἀλλ' ἡ Πολύμνια ἦτο μακρὰν ἀποῦσα. Μόνον περὶ τὰ μέσα τοῦ Αὐγούστου, ὅτε τὸ τρίτον καὶ ὀγκωδέστατον τῶν ναυπηγηθέντων πλοίων εἶχε τελειώσει ἤδη, ἐπῆγες καὶ σὺ μετὰ πολλοῦ πλήθους εἰς τὸ ναυπηγεῖον, ὅπως ἴδῃς τὴν καθέλκυσιν τοῦ μεγάλου σκάφους. Τὸ θέαμα ἦτο ἐπιβλητικόν, ὅπως λέγουσι σήμερον. Ὅλη ἡ πολίχνη εἶχεν ἐρημωθῆ σχεδόν, καὶ κόσμος πολυάριθμος ἐπλήρου τὴν μεγάλην μεταξὺ τῆς λίμνης καὶ τοῦ λιμένος λωρίδα. Ἐκεῖθεν τοῦ σκάφους, ὁ ἥλιος ἦτο ἤδη δύο κοντάρια ὑψηλά, καὶ ἵσταντο οἱ τραχεῖς, οἱ σκληραγωγημένοι ναῦται καὶ χειρώνακτες, συμπληροῦντες τὸ παλάμισμα τῆς καρίνας, ἀποκαρφώνοντες τὰ *βάζια* ἢ ὑποσκάπτοντες εἰς τὴν βάσιν, ὅπως εἶναι ἕτοιμα πρὸς πτῶσιν τὰ κοντοστύλια. Ἐντεῦθεν τοῦ σκάφους, ὅπου βαθμηδὸν ἠλαττοῦτο ἡ σκιά, ἵσταντο, πλὴν τῶν συνεργατῶν τῆς καθελκύσεως, καὶ οἱ θεαταί, καὶ οὐκ ὀλίγαι γυναῖκες, ἐλθοῦσαι πρὸς τέρψιν. Ὁποῖος τότε παλμὸς διέσεισε τὰ στήθη σου, ὅταν, μεταξὺ αὐτῶν, ἀνεγνώρισες, ὑπὸ κοκκίνην ὀμβρέλαν, τὴν περικαλλῆ μορφὴν τῆς Πολυμνίας! Εἶχεν ἐπιστρέψει ἀπὸ τὸ ταξίδιον χωρὶς νὰ τὸ μάθῃς. Ὁ Χριστοδουλής, ὅστις ἐπῆγε μὲ τὴν βάρκαν εἰς τὸ ἀτμόπλοιον, τὴν εἶχεν ἰδεῖ, ἀλλὰ δὲν σοῦ τὸ εἶπε. Καὶ ὅμως, ἠσθάνθης εἰς τὰ ἐνδόμυχά σου κρυφὸν καὶ ἀνεξομολόγητον εὐτυχίας αἴσθημα, ὅταν τὴν ἐπανεῖδες!

Ἐν τούτοις τὸ παλάμισμα εἶχε συμπληρωθῆ, τὰ βάζια ἦσαν ὅλα καρφωμένα, ἡ σκάρα μὲ τὰ βουβὰ λίπος ἀλειμμένα, ἦτο στρωμένη πρὸ πολλοῦ. Ὁ πρωτομάστορης μὲ τὸν βαριὸν ἔκαμε τοὺς νενομισμένους τρεῖς σταυροὺς εἰς τὸ πηδάλιον, καὶ ἔδωκε τὸν πρῶτον κτύπον τῆς ὠθήσεως εἰς τὸ πελώριον σκάφος. Συγχρόνως ἔπεσαν ἐν ἀκαρεῖ τὰ κοντοστύλια ὅλα. Ἡ καπετάνισσα, ὡραία, μελαγχροινή, μικρόσωμος, φορέσασα ὡς νέα ἀκόμη, διὰ τὴν περίστασιν, πλήρη τὴν νυμφικὴν στολήν της, μὲ τὸ λευκὸν ἀναφὲς καὶ αἰθερόπλαστον ἀλέμι, τὴν

as the widow of a commander in the Royal Hellenic Navy. Three large ships had been on the stocks since early March, and you had never ceased to run to the boatyard every day, often stopping for hours near the windmill, sitting on the masts that had once belonged to a schooner but were now lying on the ground, recalling that on this very spot Polymnia had stood some months before, when she had asked you to gather narcissi for her; but Polymnia was far away.

It was not until about the middle of August that the third and largest of the boats being built was completed, and you went to the boatyard with a large crowd to see the launch of the great ship. It was an impressive spectacle, as they say nowadays. The town was almost completely deserted, and the strip of land between the lagoon and the harbour was thronged with people. Beyond the ship the sun was already high, and the rough, hardened sailors and workmen were completing the tarring of the keel, driving the last nails into the slipway or digging underneath the base of the stocks so that they would be ready to fall away. On the near side of the ship, where the shade was gradually diminishing, in addition to the men helping with the launch stood the spectators, including quite a number of women who had come to enjoy themselves. How your pulse quickened when, among them, you recognized, under a red parasol, the beautiful figure of Polymnia! She had returned from her journey without your knowing. Christodoulis, who had gone out to the steamship in a dinghy, had seen her, but hadn't told you. Yet, in the depths of your being, you felt a secret and inexpressible sense of happiness when you saw her again!

In the meantime the tarring had been completed, the struts had all been nailed in place, and the slipway, with its great unhewn timbers well greased, had already been laid down. The master shipbuilder made the customary sign of the cross on the rudder three times with the sledgehammer, and dealt the first blow to get the huge ship moving. The supports all fell away in a trice. The captain's wife, a beautiful, dark-haired, slightly-built woman who, as she was still young, had put on her full bridal

χρυσοκέντητον σκούφιαν, εἰκονίζουσαν γάστραν μὲ ἄνθη καὶ μὲ κλῶνας, τὸ βελούδινον βαβουκλὶ μὲ τὰ χρυσοΰφαντα προμάνικα ἀνασηκωμένα, τὴν βυσσινόχρουν ὁλομέταξον καὶ χρυσοκέντητον τραχηλιάν, τὴν ζώνην μὲ τ' ἀργυρᾶ καὶ μαλαμοκαπνισμένα τσαπράκια, τὸ φουστάνι τὸ χαρένιο μὲ τὸ ὁλόχρυσον ποδογύρι τρεῖς σπιθαμὲς πλατύ, κρατοῦσα μέγαν ἐπάργυρον δίσκον διὰ τῆς ἀριστερᾶς, περιῆλθεν ὁλόγυρα τὸ πλοῖον καὶ ἔρρανε διὰ τῆς δεξιᾶς, μὲ κοφέτα καὶ μὲ ὀρύζιον, τὴν πρῶραν, τὴν πρύμνην, τὴν τρόπιν καὶ τὰς πλευρὰς τοῦ σκάφους. Οἱ ναῦται, οἱ ναυπηγοὶ καὶ πολλοὶ τῶν θεατῶν, ὡς σταφυλαὶ εἰς κλῆμα, ὡς μολυβῆθραι ἐπὶ σαγήνης ἁλιευτικῆς, ἐπιάσθησαν ἀπὸ τὸ παλάγκο, καὶ ἤρχισαν νὰ σύρωσι τὸν χονδρὸν κάλων νεύοντες ὅλοι πρὸς τὴν θάλασσαν, ἐπαναλαμβάνοντες ἐν ῥυθμῷ τὸ κέλευσμα: «Ἔ! γιάσαλέσα! Ἔ! γιούργια!» Ἐν τούτοις, εἴτε διότι τὸ ἔδαφος, ἐφ' οὗ εἶχε σκαρωθῆ τὸ πλοῖον, δὲν ἦτο ἀρκετὰ κατωφερές, εἴτε διὰ τὴν ἀτέλειαν τῶν κινητηρίων μέσων, τὸ σκάφος, ἐστέναζεν, ἐστέναζε, καὶ δὲν ἐκινεῖτο. Παρῆλθον ὀλίγα λεπτά, ἡ δύναμις ἐδιπλασιάσθη· ὁ μέγας ὄγκος ἐκινήθη ὀλίγον ἕως δύο σπιθαμές, τὸ παλάγκον ἐκόπη ἀπὸ τὴν βίαν τοῦ ἑλκυσμοῦ, ἡ γούμενα μὲ τοὺς δύο μακαράδες ἔμεινεν ἄπρακτος περὶ τὴν πρύμνην, οἱ ἡμίσεις τῶν ἀνθρώπων δυσμόθεν τοῦ σκάφους ἔπεσαν εἰς τὴν ἄμμον πρὸς τὸ μέρος τῆς θαλάσσης καὶ οἱ ἄλλοι ἡμίσεις ἔμειναν μὲ τὸ παλάγκον εἰς τὰς χεῖρας πρὸς τὸ μέρος τῆς λίμνης, καγχασμοὶ καὶ γογγυσμοὶ τῶν πεσόντων, ὧν τινες ἐμωλωπίσθησαν ἐλαφρῶς εἰς τὸν δεξιὸν βραχίονα ἢ τὴν πλευράν, ὁ πλοίαρχος κάθιδρως, ἡλιοκαής, ἀξιολύπητος, ἐστενοχωρεῖτο φοβερά, καὶ ὁ καπετὰν Δημήτρης ὁ Κασσανδριανός, ὅστις μὲ τὸ τσιμπούκι του, μὲ τὸν ἠλέκτρινον μαμέν, μὲ τὸ τσόχινον πανωβράκι του, μὲ τὰ ὑψηλὰ μέχρι τοῦ γόνατος ὑποδήματά του, τὰ ὁποῖα ἠγάπα νὰ φορῇ χειμῶνα καὶ θέρος, εἶχεν ἔλθει νὰ πρωτοστατήσῃ εἰς τὴν καθέλκυσιν τοῦ σκάφους, καὶ δὲν εἶχε παύσει ἀπὸ πρωίας νὰ δίδῃ ὁδηγίας καὶ συμβουλάς, ἰδὼν τὸ ἀτύχημα ἐστέναξε καὶ βραδύγλωσσος ἐπεφώνησε:

— Πφού! σκ˜λη κομυρμηγκότρυπα!

Ἐν τῷ μεταξὺ εἶχαν ἀμματίσει τὸ παλάγκο, καὶ πάλιν νέα προσπάθεια κατεβλήθη. Ἀλλὰ δὲν παρῆλθον ὀλίγα λεπτὰ καὶ τὸ παλάγκο ἐκόπη εἰς ἄλλο μέρος, ὄχι ἐκεῖ ὅπου τὸ εἶχαν ἀρτίως ἀμματίσει. Ἔφεραν νέον παλάγκο, ἐνῷ ὁ πλοίαρχος, μὴ εὐκαιρῶν νὰ σπογγίσῃ τὸν ἱδρῶτα τοῦ

costume for the occasion, with her ethereal white silk kerchief, her bonnet with its gold-embroidered pot of flowers and sprays, her velvet dress with its sleeves, woven with gold thread, slightly rolled up, her gold- embroidered crimson silk jabot, her belt with its silver gilded studs, her silk skirt with its gold hem three spans wide, holding a silver-plated tray in her left hand, walked all round the ship, showering sugared almonds and rice on the bow, the stern, the keel and the sides of the vessel with her right hand. The sailors, the builders and many of the spectators, like grapes on a vine or lead weights on a drag-net, grasped the hoist and began to pull the thick cable, all of them nodding towards the sea and repeating in rhythm the command, 'Heave away! Heave ho!' However, either because the ground on which the ship had been built did not slope down enough, or because of some imperfection in the hauling mechanism, the ship groaned and groaned, but did not budge. A few moments passed, and the haulers redoubled their efforts. The huge bulk moved a little, about two spans, but the hoist broke under the strain, the cable and the two pulleys hung useless near the stern, those of the men who were on the west side of the ship fell on the sand towards the sea, while the others remained holding the cable on the lagoon side. There was much groaning and guffawing from those who had fallen, some of whom had suffered slight bruises on their right arms or ribs, and the sunburnt captain, bathed in sweat and generally in a pitiful state, was horribly upset, while Captain Dimitris Kassandrianos, who, with his pipe with its amber mouthpiece, his coarse woollen breeches, and his knee-high boots which he liked to wear all the year round, had come to preside at the launch and since early morning had not stopped giving orders and advice, on seeing the accident, sighed and shouted in his lisping way:

'Pfui! It's nothing but a nest of worms and ants!'

In the meantime the hoist had been spliced, and a new effort was made. But a few moments later the hoist broke in a different place. A new one was brought, while the captain, too preoccupied to mop the sweat from his brow, could not but

προσώπου του, δὲν ἠδυνήθη νὰ μὴ ἐνθυμηθῇ τὴν στιγμὴν ἐκείνην τὴν ἀκούσιον ἐκείνην ἀρὰν «*Καλὸ μπλέξιμο!*» καὶ βεβαίως ἂν εἶχεν ἐμπρός του, αὐτὴν τὴν φοράν, τὸν Ἀλέξανδρον τὸν Χάραυλον, κακὸ μπλέξιμο θὰ εἶχε μαζί του. Ὁ δὲ καπετὰν Δημήτρης μὲ τὸ τσιμπούκι του, ἱστάμενος παρὰ τὴν καλύβην τοῦ γύφτου, κάτωθεν τῆς πρύμνης, ἐπανελάμβανε:

— Πφού! σκ˜ληκομυρμηγκότρυπα...

Οἱ δύο ἱερεῖς, πρώην ναυτικοί, οἵτινες εἶχαν ἀναρρίψει τὰ ἐπιτραχήλια ἐπὶ τὸν δεξιὸν ὦμον, καὶ εἶχαν ἀναβῆ ἐλαφροὶ εἰς τὸ κατάστρωμα, τελειώσαντες τὸν ἁγιασμόν, ἐπλησίασαν εἰς τὴν κωπαστὴν κ' ἔβλεπαν τὰ συμβαίνοντα, διότι, καταρριφθείσης ἤδη καὶ τῆς προχείρου κλίμακος, ἔμελλον νὰ μείνωσι ἐπὶ τοῦ πλοίου, καὶ δὲν θὰ κατέβαιναν πρὶν πέσῃ τὸ πλοῖον εἰς τὴν θάλασσαν, καὶ δυνηθῶσι νὰ κατέλθωσι, μὲ τὰς ἱερὰς εἰκόνας, εἰς τὴν βάρκαν. Πλῆθος δὲ ἀπὸ *ἀθερίνες* — παιδία ὀκταετῆ καὶ δεκαετῆ — ἔτρεχαν ἐμπρὸς ὀπίσω ἐπὶ τοῦ καταστρώματος, βοηθοῦντα διὰ τοῦ μέσου τούτου εἰς τὴν καθέλκυσιν τοῦ πλοίου.

Τέλος, μετὰ πολλοὺς ἀγῶνας, καὶ τῇ ἐφαρμογῇ πολλῶν θεραπευτικῶν μέσων, τὸ μέγα πλοῖον, ἀργὰ ἀργά, ὡς καμαρωμένη νύμφη, ἔπεσεν εἰς τὴν θάλασσαν. Μέγας τότε ὁ ἀλαλαγμός, γυναικῶν σταυροκοπουμένων, παιδίων σκιρτώντων, ἀνδρῶν τρεχόντων ὀπίσω τῆς πρύμνης ὡς νὰ ἤθελον διὰ τοῦ δρόμου τούτου νὰ ἐκπτοήσωσι καὶ νὰ πειθαναγκάσωσι τὸ πλοῖον νὰ πέσῃ εἰς τὴν θάλασσαν. Καὶ ὁ μέγας καραβόσκυλος, ὁ Τσοῦρμος, τρέχων καὶ αὐτὸς ὅσον τοῦ ἐπέτρεπεν ἡ ἄκρα ἔντασις τῆς ἁλύσεώς του, ἐγαύγιζε μανιωδῶς προπέμπων τὸ πλοῖον ἐφ' οὗ ἐντὸς τῆς ἡμέρας ἔμελλε νὰ μεταφερθῇ. Καὶ ἐνῷ ὅλοι ἔτρεχαν πρὸς τὴν θάλασσαν κατόπιν τοῦ ὀλισθαίνοντος καὶ καταφερομένου διὰ τῆς ἐσχάρας σκάφους, εἷς μόνος ἐστράφη αἴφνης, κρατῶν τὸν βαριόν του, καὶ ἔτρεξε πρὸς τὴν ἀντίθετον διεύθυνσιν, πρὸς τὴν ξηράν, ὡς διὰ νὰ κρυβῇ εἰς τὴν καλύβην τοῦ πλοιάρχου, τὴν χρησιμεύουσαν ὡς ἀποθήκην καὶ διὰ τὸν ὕπνον τοῦ νυκτερινοῦ φύλακος. Ὁ τρέχων οὕτως ἦτο αὐτὸς ὁ πρωτομάστορης, καὶ ἔτρεχεν οὐχὶ δι' ἄλλον λόγον, ἢ διὰ νὰ μὴ συμμερισθῇ τὸ λουτρὸν τοῦ πλοιάρχου, τὸ ὁποῖον τινὲς ἐζήτουν κατ' ἔθος νὰ ἐπεκτείνωσι καὶ εἰς αὐτόν. Ἠκούσθη δὲ τότε αἴφνης μεγάλη φωνή, δεσπόσασα ὅλου τοῦ παμμιγοῦς θορύβου:

— Τὸν καπετάνιο στὸ γιαλό!

Ἡ φωνὴ αὕτη ἐξῆλθεν ἐκ πολλῶν στομάτων συγχρόνως. Ὁ

remember the unintentional curse, 'Good failing!' If he had seen Alexandros Charavlos in front of him this time, he would certainly have given him a good flailing. Captain Dimitris, with his pipe, standing next to the gypsy's hut below the stern, repeated:

'Pfui! It's nothing but a nest of worms and ants!'

The two priests — former sailors — who had thrown their stoles over their right shoulders and leapt lightly on to the deck and performed the blessing, came over to the gunwale to see what was happening, because, the makeshift ladder having by now collapsed, they were about to be left on board the ship, unable either to disembark before it slipped into the sea or to get down into the dinghy with their holy icons. Meanwhile a crowd of small fry — children of eight and nine — ran up and down the deck in an attempt to launch the ship.

Finally, after many efforts and by the application of many remedial measures, the great ship, like a proud bride, gradually slipped into the sea. There were great whoops of joy from women repeatedly crossing themselves, children leaping about, and men running behind the stern as though trying to intimidate the ship and force it to slide into the water. Tsourmos, the big ship's dog, who was also running about as much as the extreme tension of his chain would allow, barked frenziedly to send off the ship on which within the day he would embark. While everyone else was running towards the sea behind the ship as it slid down the slipway, one man suddenly turned round, holding his sledgehammer, and ran in the other direction, away from the sea, as if to hide in the captain's hut, which had been used as a storehouse and sleeping-quarters by the night-watchman. The man who was running was the master shipbuilder, and he was running for no other reason than to avoid sharing the captain's dunking, which some people were seeking, according to custom, to extend to him too. For at that moment a great cry arose above the multifarious other noises:

'Into the sea with the captain!'

The cry came from many mouths at the same time. Captain

καπετὰν Γιωργάκης, ἐνδίδων εἰς τὴν ἀπαίτησιν τοῦ πλήθους, ἀπορρίψας τὰ ἐλαφρὰ ὑποδήματά του, ἔτρεξεν ἐπὶ τῆς σκάρας, πατῶν ἐπὶ τῶν ὀνύχων, ὄπισθεν τῆς πρύμνης, καὶ τὴν στιγμὴν καθ' ἣν ἡ πρύμνη ἀπηλλάσσετο τέλος τῆς ἐσχάρας καὶ τὸ σκάφος, φέρον ὑπερήφανον τὴν κυανόλευκον ἐπὶ κονταρίου μετ' ἐρυθροῦ σταυροῦ, ἐβαπτίζετο τὸ πρῶτον εἰς τὸ κῦμα, ἐρρίφθη μὲ ὅλα τὰ ἐνδύματά του κατὰ κεφαλῆς εἰς τὴν θάλασσαν, βυθισθεὶς πρῶτον, εἶτα εὐθὺς ἀνελθὼν εἰς τὴν ἐπιφάνειαν, καὶ ἀφοῦ ἐκολύμβησε δύο ἢ τρεῖς γύρες, ἐπέστρεψεν εἰς τὰ ρηχά, ἐπάτησεν εἰς τὴν ἄμμον, ἀπέβη εἰς τὴν ξηράν, καὶ ὑπὸ τοὺς ἀλαλαγμοὺς τοῦ πλήθους ἔτρεξεν εἰς τὴν καλύβην ὅπου εἰς τὴν στιγμὴν ἤλλαξε τὰ βρεγμένα ἀμπαδίτικα κ' ἐφόρεσε τὰ κυριακάτικα.

Εἰς ὅλα ταῦτα ἦσο παρών, φίλε, καὶ ὅλα σχεδὸν δὲν τὰ ἔβλεπες. Ἡ καρδία σου, ἡ φαντασία σου, οἱ ὀφθαλμοί σου ἦσαν προσκεκολλημένα εἰς ἐκείνην ἥτις ἐφόρει τότε λινομέταξον θερινὴν ἐσθῆτα κ' ἐσκιάζετο ἀπὸ τὸ κόκκινον παρασόλι. Μόνον οἱ ἀλαλαγμοὶ τοῦ πλήθους σὲ ἀπέσπασαν ἀπὸ τῆς βυθίας θεωρίας σου, ὅταν τὸ πλοῖον εἶχε πέσει εἰς τὴν θάλασσαν, καὶ ὁ πλοίαρχος ἔγινεν ὑποβρύχιος κατόπιν αὐτοῦ. Ἀλλ' ἅπαξ ἐξυπνήσας, εἶδες, φεῦ! καί τι ἄλλο, τὸ ὁποῖον πολλοὶ τῶν παρεστώτων δὲν παρετήρησαν. Κατόπιν τοῦ πλοιάρχου, τρέξας, μετ' ἀλλοκότου ἐνθουσιασμοῦ, ῥήξας κραυγὴν ἡδονῆς καὶ θριάμβου, ἐρρίφθη εἰς τὴν θάλασσαν νέος τις, μόλις δεκαπενταέτης. Ἦτο ὁ Κ'στοδουλής, ὁ παιδικὸς φίλος σου. Πόθεν ἄρα ὡρμήθη νὰ τὸ κάμῃ; Ἴσως διότι ἤλπιζε διὰ τῆς ἐθελοθυσίας ταύτης, τῆς προσφερομένης εἰς τὴν φειδωλὴν Μοῖραν, ν' ἀξιωθῇ νὰ γίνῃ καὶ αὐτὸς πλοίαρχος μίαν ἡμέραν; Ἴσως καὶ ἁπλῶς διὰ νὰ τὸν ἰδῇ ἡ Πολύμνια; Οὔτε τὸ ἓν οὔτε τὸ ἄλλο. Ὁ Χριστοδουλὴς εἶχεν ἔλθει ὀλίγον ἀργὰ εἰς τὸ ναυπηγεῖον, ὅταν εἶχεν ἀφαιρεθῇ ἡ σανὶς ἡ χρησιμεύουσα ὡς κλῖμαξ καὶ αἱ ἀντηρίδες εἶχαν ἤδη ὑποσκαφῆ. Ἠσθάνετο δὲ ἀκατανίκητον ἐπιθυμίαν ν' ἀναβῇ εἰς τὸ καράβι. Τί νὰ κάμῃ; Δὶς καὶ τρὶς ἐδοκίμασε νὰ προσκολληθῇ πότε εἰς ἓν πότε εἰς ἄλλο κοντοστύλι, ἂς ἦτο καὶ ἡ βάσις τῶν ἐπισφαλής, καὶ ν' ἀναρριχηθῇ τολμηρῶς ἕως τὴν κωπαστὴν τοῦ καραβιοῦ. Δὶς καὶ τρὶς τὸν εἶδον, πότε ὁ πρωτομάστορης, πότε εἷς τῶν μαραγκῶν, καὶ μετ' αὐστηρότητος τὸν ἐμπόδισαν. Τότε τί νὰ κάμῃ καὶ αὐτός; Ἀφοῦ δὲν ἠξιώθη ν' ἀναβῇ ἐγκαίρως εἰς τὸ πλοῖον, ἐπαρηγορήθη ριφθεὶς εἰς τὴν

Yorgakis, giving in to the crowd's demands, threw off his light shoes and ran on tiptoe along the slipway behind the stern, and the moment the stern at last slid free of the slipway and the ship, proudly flying the blue-and-white Greek flag from a pole topped by a red cross, received its first baptism, he threw himself, fully clothed, headlong into the sea, first sinking and then immediately re-emerging at the surface, and after swimming around the ship two or three times, returned to the shallow water, stood on the sandy bottom, came out on to dry land and to the accompaniment of whoops of excitement from the crowd ran to the hut, where in a trice he changed out of his wet coarse woollens into his Sunday best.

You were present at all this, my friend, yet you saw scarcely anything of it. Your heart, your fancy, your eyes were riveted on the girl who wore a linen and silk summer dress and was shaded by a red parasol. It was only the shouts of the crowd when the ship slipped into the sea and the captain had plunged into the water after it that aroused you from your deep meditations. But once you had awoken you saw something else, alas, which many of the bystanders did not notice. Running excitedly behind the captain with a shriek of delight and triumph, a young lad of just fifteen years old threw himself into the sea. It was Christodoulis, your childhood friend. What could have driven him to do this? Did he hope that by offering up this willing sacrifice to parsimonious Fate he would one day be fortunate enough to become a captain himself? Or was it simply that he wanted Polymnia to see him? It was neither of these things. Christodoulis had arrived rather late at the boatyard, when the plank serving as a gangway had been removed and the supports had been dug away. He felt an indomitable desire to climb on to the ship. But what could he do? Two or three times he tried to grab hold of one or other of the supports, even though they stood so precariously, and climb boldly up to the gunwale of the ship. Each time either the master shipbuilder or one of the carpenters saw him and vigorously prevented him. Then what could he do? Since he had not been lucky enough to board the ship in time, he

θάλασσαν καὶ ἀκολουθήσας τὸ σκάφος εἰς τὸν δρόμον του. Ἐν τούτοις σὺ ἠσθάνθης πικρὸν νυγμὸν ζηλοτυπίας. Ἡ καρδία σου ἐπληγώθη ἀπὸ τὸ παιδαριῶδες τοῦτο κατόρθωμα. Πτωχὸς Χριστοδουλής! Τί τοῦ εἶχεν ἔλθει; Καὶ οὔτε ἐξῆλθεν εἰς τὴν ξηρὰν διὰ ν' ἀλλάξῃ, ὅπου ἄλλως δὲν θὰ εὕρισκεν ἐνδύματα, ἀλλ' ἠκολούθησε κολυμβῶν τὸ ἀπομακρυνθὲν πλοῖον, μὲ τὸ ὑποκάμισον καὶ τὴν περισκελίδα φουσκωμένα ὡς πανία βάρκας, ὑπεράνω τῆς ἐπιφανείας τῆς θαλάσσης, εἶτα δὲ ἀνελθὼν εἰς λέμβον, ἐζήτησε διὰ νευμάτων ἀπὸ τοὺς ἐπὶ τοῦ πλοίου θριαμβευτικῶς ἀλαλάζοντας παῖδας νὰ τοῦ ῥίψωσιν ἐνδύματα· μικρὸς μοῦτσος, εὐσπλαγχνισθείς, τοῦ ἔρριψεν ὑποκάμισον καὶ περισκελίδα ἰδικά του, καὶ ὁ Χριστοδουλής, ἀφοῦ ἤλλαξε, προσεκολλήθη εἰς μίαν τῶν πλευρῶν, καὶ πιασθεὶς ἀπὸ σχοινίου, ἀνῆλθε θριαμβεύων εἰς τὸ ὑψηλὸν καὶ ἀνερμάτιστον σκάφος.

Τὸ πλῆθος εἰς τὸ ναυπηγεῖον συνωθεῖτο τώρα περὶ τὴν καλύβην τοῦ πλοιάρχου, ὅπου ἡ μεγαλοπρεπῶς στολισμένη καπετάνισσα μετὰ προθυμίας καὶ ἁβρότητος προσέφερεν εἰς ὅλους γλυκύσματα καὶ ποτά. Ἀλλὰ σὺ ᾐσθάνεσο τόσην πικρίαν εἰς τὸν οὐρανίσκον ὡς νὰ εἶχεν ἀναβῆ ἡ χολή σου ὅλη κ' ἐχύθη προώρως εἰς τὸ στόμα σου. Καὶ ἐπιστρέφουσαν εἰς τὴν πόλιν ἠκολούθησες μακρόθεν τὴν Πολυμνίαν, τὴν ὁποίαν εἶχες ἰδεῖ μειδιῶσαν πρὸς τὴν τρέλαν τοῦ παιδικοῦ σου φίλου, καὶ τὴν εἶχες ἀκούσει ψιθυρίζουσαν: «Τί παράξενο παιδί, αὐτὸς ὁ Χριστοδουλής!»

* * *

Δὲν ἦτο αὕτη ἡ μόνη φορὰ καθ' ἣν ὁ Χριστοδουλής ἐρρίφθη εἰς τὸ ὕδωρ μὲ ὅλα τὰ ἐνδύματά του, πρὸ τῶν ὀφθαλμῶν τῆς Πολυμνίας ἢ καὶ χάριν αὐτῆς. Ὀλίγας ἡμέρας ὕστερον, μίαν Κυριακὴν περὶ τὰ τέλη Αὐγούστου, ὁ Παρρήσης ὁ καλλιεργητὴς τοῦ σικυῶνος, καλόκαρδος, ἄφροντις, μελαψός, μὲ μακρὰν τὴν φούντα τοῦ φεσιοῦ κρεμαμένην ἐπὶ τοῦ ὤμου, καὶ ὁ Λούκας ὁ ἐκμισθωτὴς τῆς λίμνης, ὑψηλόκορμος, μὲ μακρὰ σκέλη, μὲ λινόχρουν τὸν μακρὸν πέραν τῶν ὤτων μύστακα, μὲ ἀστακοῦ βρασμένου τὸν χρῶτα τοῦ προσώπου, εἶχαν καθίσει καθὼς πολὺ συχνὰ τὸ ἐσυνήθιζαν «νὰ τὸ κλάψουν» ὀλίγον, παρὰ τὸ χεῖλος τῆς λίμνης, ὑπὸ τὴν δροσερὰν ἀναδενδράδα, ἔξωθεν τῆς καλύβης των. Ὁ ἥλιος ἔκλινε πρὸς τὴν δύσιν, καὶ ἀπὸ μιᾶς ὥρας ἤδη εἶχον δώσει καὶ λάβει ἐναλλὰξ πολλοὺς ἀδελφικοὺς ἀσπασμοὺς εἰς τὰ χείλη τῆς φλάσκας, ἥτις ἦτο τετράοκαδος καὶ εἶχε

consoled himself by plunging into the sea and following in its wake. Nevertheless, you felt a bitter pang of jealousy. You were cut to the quick by this childish exploit. Poor Christodoulis! What had come over him? He didn't even come out on to the beach to change; besides, he wouldn't have found any clothes there. Instead, he swam behind the ship as it floated further and further away, his shirt and trousers billowing above the surface of the sea like a dinghy's sails; then, getting into a small boat, he signalled to the boys triumphantly shouting on board the ship to throw some clothes down to him. A small cabin-boy took pity on him and threw him a shirt and trousers of his own, and Christodoulis, having changed, came close to the side of the tall, unballasted ship, grabbed hold of a rope and hauled himself triumphantly on to the deck.

The crowd at the boatyard was still congregating round the captain's hut, where his magnificently adorned wife was eagerly and graciously handing round sweets and drinks. But you had a bitter taste on your palate, as though your bile had risen into your mouth. Polymnia, whom you had seen smiling at your young friend's escapade and whispering, 'What a strange boy that Christodoulis is!', returned to town, and you followed her at a distance.

*   *   *

This wasn't the only time that Christodoulis threw himself into the water fully clothed in front of Polymnia or for her sake. A few days later, one Sunday at the end of August, Parrisis, the melon-farmer, sunburnt, cheerful and light-hearted, the long tassel of his fez hanging down to his shoulder, and Loukas, the lagoon's tenant fisherman, tall, long-legged, his flaxen moustache projecting beyond his ears and his complexion the colour of boiled lobster, had sat down for a drink, as they very frequently did, at the edge of the lagoon under a cool trellis outside their hut. The sun was sinking, and for an hour, each taking his turn, they had already exchanged many fraternal kisses with the wine-flask, which held four okas and had recently been brought from town full of

κομισθῇ ἀρτίως ἐκ τῆς πολίχνης πλήρης μοσχάτου. Ὁ πιστὸς φίλος των, ὁ Ἀργύρης, ὁ συνιδιοκτήτης τοῦ ἀνεμομύλου, τοὺς εἶχεν ἐπισκεφθῆ πρὸ μικροῦ μὲ τὰ ἀστεῖά του, καὶ εἰς τὸν μὲν Λούκαν εἶχε προσφέρει τσιγάρον μετὰ πυρίτιδος, ὅπερ ἀνάψας ἐκεῖνος ἔκαυσεν ὀλίγον διὰ τῆς ἐκρήξεως τὸν πυρρὸν μύστακά του, καὶ ἀτάραχος εἶπε: «Ζαρὰρ γιόκ!», εἰς τὸν Παρρήσην δὲ εἶχεν ἐπιδώσει σπασμένην γκάιδαν, προτρέπων αὐτὸν «νὰ παίξῃ κανένα χαβά», ἀλλ' ὅσον καὶ ἂν ἠγωνίζετο πνευστιῶν ὁ Παρρήσης, ἡ γκάιδα οὐδένα ἐξέβαλλε φθόγγον. Τέλος, ὁ Ἀργύρης, εἶπε: «δὲ φελᾶτε τίποτε, κ' οἱ δυό σας, κρῖμα σ' ἐσᾶς, κρῖμας!» Καὶ προσποιηθεὶς δυσαρέσκειαν ἀπῆλθεν. Οἱ δύο φίλοι ἔμειναν μόνοι ἐξακολουθοῦντες νὰ ἐκκενῶσι σιγὰ σιγὰ καὶ μεθοδικῶς τὴν φλάσκαν. Εἶχαν ψήσει εἰς ἀνθρακιὰν ἡμίσειαν δωδεκάδα κεφαλόπουλα, καὶ οὐκ ὀλίγα καβούρια, καὶ τὸ μοσχᾶτον κατέβαινε μιὰ χαρὰ κάτω. Εἶχαν ἐνθυμηθῆ παλαιὰς ἱστορίας, διηγοῦντο πρὸς ἀλλήλους τὰ παθήματά των, τὰ ὁποῖα δὲν εἶχον τελειωμόν. Ὁ Παρρήσης μάλιστα, ἐξαρθεὶς ἀπὸ τῆς πεζότητος, ἐτραγούδει κατὰ προτίμησιν «μερακλίδικα» τραγούδια, οἷον τὸν στίχον:

Σὰν κλῆμα μὲ κλαδεύουνε καὶ κλαδεμοὺς δὲν ἔχω...

Ἔλεγαν δὲ πρὸς ἀλλήλους: «Θυμᾶσαι, καρδάσ', τοῦτο; Θυμᾶσαι, γιολδάσ', αὐτό;» Ὅταν εἶναί τις μὲ τὸν ἄριστον φίλον του εἰς ὡραίαν ἐξοχήν, συμπαραστατούσης καὶ φλάσκας μὲ μοσχᾶτον, λησμονεῖ τὰ πάντα, καὶ οἱ δύο ἄνδρες οὐδ' ὑπώπτευαν ὅτι τοὺς ἔβλεπέ τις, ὅπερ ἄλλως τοὺς ἦτο ἀδιάφορον. Ἀλλ' ὄπισθεν τῶν καλαμώνων, ἐπὶ τῆς ἀντιπέραν ὄχθης, ἥμισυ μίλιον μακράν, ἦτο χωμένος ἀπὸ δύο ὡρῶν, ἀφανής, ὁ παιδικὸς φίλος σου, ὁ Χριστοδουλῆς. Τί ἐζήτει ἐκεῖ; Κατὰ πᾶσαν πιθανότητα παρεμόνευε πότε θ' ἀπεμακρύνοντο πρὸς στιγμὴν ἀπὸ τῆς ὄχθης ὁ Παρρήσης καὶ ὁ Λούκας, διὰ νὰ χωθῇ γοργὰ εἰς τὴν λίμνην, καὶ κλέψῃ, ὁ πονηρός, κανένα ἔγχελυν ἢ κεφαλόπουλά τινα καὶ ὀλίγα καβούρια. Ἀλλὰ μάτην ἐπερίμενε, καὶ ἤδη εἶχεν ἀποφασίσει, ἀναγνωρίσας μακρόθεν τὴν τσότραν καὶ ἐλπίζων ὅτι οἱ δύο φίλοι, ἐν τῇ εὐθυμίᾳ των, δὲν θὰ τὸν ἔβλεπον, νὰ ἐπιχειρήσῃ τὸ τόλμημα καὶ ἀπέναντι αὐτῶν. Ἀλλὰ τὴν στιγμὴν ἐκείνην ἀπροσδόκητον συμβὰν εἵλκυσε τὴν προσοχήν του.

Ἤγγιζεν ὁ ἥλιος εἰς τὴν δύσιν, ὅταν εἰς τὴν καλύβην, ἔξωθεν τῆς

moschato.* Their faithful friend Argyris, the joint-owner of the windmill, had just visited them and entertained them with his pranks, giving Loukas a cigarette containing gunpowder, which made a slight explosion that singed his reddish moustache when he lit it, after which he said quite calmly, '*Zarar yok!*'* Argyris had given Parrisis a broken set of bagpipes, urging him to play a tune, but, much as he exerted himself with his puffing, the instrument refused to let out a sound. Finally Argyris said, 'You're no good for anything, the pair of you, it's a crying shame!' So saying, he walked off with feigned displeasure. The two friends remained there alone and continued to drain the flask slowly and methodically. They had grilled half a dozen grey mullet and no small number of crabs on the charcoal, and the *moschato* was going down a treat. They reminisced, telling each other of their sufferings, of which there was no end. Indeed Parrisis, rising above the level of the prosaic, was moved to sing fanciful songs, such as:

They try to prune me, but I won't be pruned...

Each of them kept saying to the other, 'D'you remember that, chum? D'you remember that?' When one is with one's best friend in a lovely spot in the countryside, one forgets everything with the help of a flask of *moschato*, and the two men little suspected that someone could see them — besides, they couldn't have cared less. But half a mile away, behind the reeds on the far bank, your childhood friend Christodoulis had been lurking unobserved for two hours. What was he after? In all probability the cunning lad was biding his time until Parrisis and Loukas left the shore for a moment, so that he could plunge into the lagoon and steal an eel or some grey mullet and a few crabs. But he had waited in vain, and, having espied the wine-flask and hoping that the two friends would be too merry to notice, he had already decided to carry out the escapade in front of their eyes. But at that moment an unexpected incident attracted his attention.

The sun was setting when a woman accompanied by a boy

ὁποίας ἐκάθηντο οἱ δύο συμπόται, ἐπλησίασε γυνή τις συνοδευομένη ὑπὸ μειρακίου. Ἐφόρει λευκὴν ἐσθῆτα κ' ἐκράτει κόκκινον παρασόλι, καὶ ὁ Χριστοδουλῆς μὲ ὅλην τὴν ἀπόστασιν, τὴν ἀνεγνώρισεν εὐθύς. Ἦτο ἡ Πολύμνια μετὰ τοῦ ἀδελφοῦ της, τοῦ Νίκου. Οἱ δύο ἄνδρες ἐσηκώθησαν εὐθύς, κ' ἐκ τῶν νευμάτων καὶ ὑποκλίσεών των, ἐνόησεν ὁ Χριστοδουλῆς, χωμένος μέσα εἰς τὲς καλαμιές, ὅτι τὴν ἐπεριποιοῦντο καὶ ἦσαν πρόθυμοι εἰς τοὺς ὁρισμούς της. Ὀλίγαι παρῆλθον στιγμαί, καὶ βλέπει τὴν Πολύμνιαν νὰ πηδήσῃ καὶ νὰ ἐπιβῇ εἰς τὴν μικρὰν φελούκαν, εἶδος σκάφης μ' ἐπίπεδον τὸ κύτος, χωρὶς καρίναν, ἥτις ἦτο δεδεμένη εἰς τὸ χεῖλος τῆς λίμνης, οὐ μακρὰν τῆς καλύβης, καὶ ἧς ἐπιβαίνων ὁ Λούκας ἐθήρευεν ἀνὰ τὴν λίμνην τοὺς ἐγχέλεις — καὶ — τὰ κεφαλόπουλα. Κατόπιν τῆς νεάνιδος, ὁ μικρὸς ἀδελφός της, λύσας τὴν μπαρούμα, ἐπέβη, καὶ λαβὼν τὸ κοντάριον, ἤρχισε ν' ἀβαράρῃ εἰς τὸν βυθὸν τῆς ἀβαθοῦς λίμνης. Ὁ Χριστοδουλῆς ἐσυμπέρανεν ὀρθῶς ὅτι τῆς Πολυμνίας θὰ τῆς εἶχεν ἔλθει ἡ φαντασία νὰ κάμῃ μίαν φορὰν μὲ τὴν φελούκαν περίπατον ἐπὶ τῆς λίμνης, καὶ ὁ Λούκας, εὐδιάθετος εὑρεθείς, τῆς ἔδωκε τὴν ἄδειαν.

Ἡ μικρὰ σκάφη ἀπεμακρύνθη πρὸς τὸ κέντρον τῆς λίμνης, οἱ δύο ἄνδρες καθίσαντες ἐκ νέου, ἠσχολοῦντο ν' ἀποτελειώσουν τὴν φλάσκαν, καὶ ὁ Χριστοδουλῆς κρυμμένος εἰς τοὺς καλαμῶνας, ἔβλεπε θαυμάζων, ὅπως θὰ ἐθαύμαζες σύ, τὸ χαριέστατον σύμπλεγμα τῆς νεάνιδος καὶ τοῦ μικροῦ ἀδελφοῦ της, ἐξακολουθοῦντος, μὲ ὅλην του τὴν δύναμιν, διὰ τοῦ κονταρίου ν' ἀντωθῇ τὸν πυθμένα. Ἡ Πολύμνια ἐφαίνετο ἀκτινοβολοῦσα ἐκ χαρᾶς. Ὁ περίπατος οὗτος τὴν ηὔφραινε, τὴν κατεγοήτευεν, ὡς τὰ ἀθύρματα τὰς τριετεῖς κορασίδας, ἐνῷ ὁ ἀδελφός της ἐφαίνετο αἰσθανόμενος ἴσην χαρὰν μὲ τὰ ἑπταετῆ παιδία, τὰ ὁποῖα φεύγοντα τὸ σχολεῖον, μὲ τὸν *φύλακα* ἀνηρτημένον ὑπὸ τὴν μασχάλην, εὑρίσκουσιν ἄφατον ἡδονὴν νὰ τρέχουν εἰς τὲς ἀκρογιαλιὲς καὶ εἰς τοὺς βάλτους, καὶ νὰ *καραβίζουν* μὲ σμικρότατα κομψὰ καραβάκια, τὰ ὁποῖα οἱ ἐπιδεξιώτεροι μεταξύ των κατασκευάζουσιν. Ὁ Χριστοδουλῆς ἐλησμόνησε τὰ χέλια, τὰ καβουράκια καὶ τὰ κεφαλόπουλα, τὰ ὁποῖα διενοεῖτο νὰ κλέψῃ, καὶ δὲν ἐχόρταινε νὰ βλέπῃ τὴν παιδικὴν ἐκείνην ἐπὶ τῆς λίμνης περιπλάνησιν. Ἀλλὰ δὲν τοῦ διέφυγε καὶ ἡ *ἀτζαμωσύνη* τοῦ Νίκου, ὅστις δὲν ἤξευρε ν' *ἀβαράρῃ* κανονικὰ καθὼς ἔπρεπε, καὶ χωμένος μέσα εἰς τοὺς καλαμῶνας ὁ παιδικὸς φίλος σου ἐστέναζε κ' ἔλεγεν: «Ἄ! νὰ ἤμουν ἐγώ!... »

approached the hut, outside which the two topers were sitting. She was wearing a white dress and holding a red parasol, and Christodoulis, despite the distance, recognized her immediately. It was Polymnia with her brother Nikos. The two men stood up immediately, and Christodoulis, lurking in the reeds, understood from their gestures and their bows that they were welcoming her courteously and seeing to her every bidding. A few moments passed, and he saw Polymnia jump into a small punt, a craft with a flat bottom and no keel, which was moored at the edge of the lagoon not far from the hut and which Loukas used for catching eels and grey mullet in the lagoon. Behind the young woman, her little brother, untying the mooring-rope, stepped into the craft and, grasping the pole, began to thrust it into the bottom of the shallow lagoon. Christodoulis concluded rightly that Polymnia must have conceived a fancy to go punting on the lake for once in her life, and Loukas, being in a good mood, had given her permission.

The small craft moved away towards the middle of the lagoon, while the two men sat down again and occupied themselves with the task of emptying the flask. Christodoulis, hidden in the reeds, watched in admiration, as you would have done, the charming scene of the young woman and her brother, who continued to thrust the pole into the bottom with all his might. Polymnia seemed radiant with joy. She was delighted and captivated by this excursion, like a three-year-old girl with her toys, while her brother seemed to be as happy as those seven-year-old boys who, leaving school with their satchels slung over their shoulders, find inexpressible delight in running to the beach and the marshes to sail neat little toy boats made by the more skilful among them. Christodoulis forgot the eels, the crabs and the grey mullet that he was planning to steal, entranced at the sight of the two young people gliding across the lagoon. But he could not fail to notice Nikos's ineptitude at pushing the pole in smoothly and regularly, and, lurking in the reeds, your childhood friend sighed and said, 'Oh, if only it was me!'

* * *

Ἐκεῖ, εἰς μίαν στιγμήν, καθὼς *ἀβαράριζεν* ἀδεξίως ὁ Νῖκος, ἡ φελούκα περιεπλάκη εἰς συστάδα λιμναίων χόρτων, ὑψηλῶν, σχεδὸν ἕως τὴν ἐπιφάνειαν, καὶ ὁ Νῖκος ἔκαμνεν, ἔκαμνε ν' ἀβαράρῃ, καὶ ὅσον ἀβαράριζε, τόσον χειρότερα περιεπλέκετο ἡ φελούκα, καὶ τὸ κοντάριον δὲν εὕρισκε πλέον πυθμένα, καὶ τέλος τὸ κοντάριον περιεπλάκη καὶ αὐτὸ εἰς τὰ πολύκλαδα, ἀδρά, μέλανα ἐκεῖνα χόρτα, καὶ ὁ Νῖκος εἰς μάτην ἐπάσχιζε ν' ἀπαλλάξῃ ἐκεῖθεν τὸ κοντάριον, καὶ ὅσον ἐτράβα ὁ Νῖκος, τόσον τὸ κοντάρι ἔφευγεν ἀπὸ τὰς χεῖράς του, ἑωσοῦ ἔπεσεν ἀπὸ τοὺς ἀσθενεῖς δακτύλους, καὶ τὸ μισὸν ἦτο ἐμπλεγμένον κάτω, τὸ μισὸν ἔπλεεν εἰς τὴν ἐπιφάνειαν. Ἡ Πολύμνια ἐγερθεῖσα μὲ προφύλαξιν ἔκυψε διὰ νὰ ἴδῃ ποῦ ἐπῆγε τὸ κοντάριον, ἀπὸ τὴν αὐτὴν πλευρὰν τῆς φελούκας, πρὸς ἣν ἵστατο καὶ ὁ Νῖκος, ἀλλὰ τότε ἡ φελούκα ἔγειρε μονόπλευρα, καὶ παρ' ὀλίγον ἀνετρέπετο. Ἐννοήσασα τὸν κίνδυνον ἡ Πολυμνία, καὶ μὴ ἐπιθυμοῦσα νὰ κάμῃ ἀκούσιον λουτρὸν μέσα εἰς τὰ λιμναῖα χόρτα, ἀνεκάθισε ταχεῖα παρὰ τὴν πρύμνην, καὶ πάλιν ὑπεγερθεῖσα ὕψωσε τὸ λευκὸν μανδήλιόν της πρὸς τοὺς δύο συμπότας τῆς μικρᾶς καλύβης καὶ συγχρόνως ἤρχισε νὰ φωνάζῃ:

—Ἔ! μπαρμπα-Λούκα!

Ἀλλ' ἕως νὰ πάρῃ εἴδησιν ὁ Λούκας καὶ ἀποφασίσῃ νὰ ἔλθῃ εἰς βοήθειαν (ὅπερ ἄλλως θὰ ἦτο δύσκολον, διότι τὸ ἔδαφος τοῦ πυθμένος ἦτο πανταχοῦ σχεδὸν βαλτῶδες καὶ πᾶς ὁ ἐπιβαίνων εἰς τὸ ὕδωρ θὰ ἐχώνετο μέχρι τοῦ γόνατος εἰς ἰλύν· τὸ ἀβαθὲς δὲ τοῦ ὕδατος δὲν ἐπέτρεπε νὰ κολυμβήσῃ μέγα σῶμα, οἷον τὸ ἰδικόν του), θὰ ἐνύκτωνε χωρὶς νὰ κατορθωθῇ τίποτε. Ἀλλ' ὁ Χριστοδουλῆς εὐτυχῶς, ὁ παιδικὸς φίλος σου, ἦτο πολὺ σιμότερα εἰς τὴν φελούκαν, ἀπὸ ἐκεῖ ὁποῦ ἦτο χωμένος, μέσα εἰς τοὺς καλαμῶνας. Χωρὶς νὰ διστάσῃ, μὲ τὸ ὑποκάμισον καὶ τὴν περισκελίδα, τὰ ὁποῖα ἀπετέλουν πάντοτε ὅλην τὴν ἐνδυμασίαν του, ἐκπηδήσας ἀπὸ τὸν καλαμῶνα, ἀπροσδοκήτως, θαυμασίως, ὡς τελευταῖον ἀπομεινάριον ἀρχαίας θεότητος, λιμναίας καὶ ὑδροβίου, ἄγνωστον καὶ νοθογενές, λησμονημένον ἀπὸ δεκαεννέα αἰώνων, διαιτώμενον ἐκεῖ εἰς τοὺς καλαμῶνας, διαφυγὸν τὴν προσοχὴν τοῦ χριστιανικοῦ κόσμου, ἐρρίφθη κολυμβῶν εἰς τὴν λίμνην. Καὶ μὲ δέκα εἰρεσίας τῶν χειρῶν, μὲ ἄλλα τόσα λακτίσματα τῶν ποδῶν, μὲ τὴν κοιλίαν θίγουσαν κάποτε εἰς τοὺς βάλτους, ἔφθασεν εἰς τὸ μέρος, ὅπου εἶχεν ἐμπλακῆ ἡ βάρκα, ἀνεπήδησε στιβαρῶς

*   *   *

Suddenly, while Nikos was punting in his clumsy way, the craft got caught in a clump of tall waterweed that almost reached the surface. He tried and tried to push with his pole, but the more he tried, the more the craft became entangled; now the pole didn't reach the bottom, and finally it too got caught in the luxuriant black weeds; Nikos struggled in vain to extricate it, but the more he pulled, the more the pole slipped out of his hands, until it finally fell from his weak fingers, half of it caught under the surface, the other half floating above. Polymnia, getting up gingerly, leant over the side where Nikos was standing to see where the pole had gone, and the boat lurched over, almost capsizing. Realizing the danger and not wishing to take an unintentional bath amongst the waterweed, Polymnia sat down again quickly near the stern and, raising herself slightly, waved her white handkerchief towards the two topers at the little hut, shouting:

'Hey, Uncle Loukas!'

But by the time Loukas had noticed and decided to come to their aid (which would have been difficult, since the bottom of the lagoon was muddy, and anyone who waded into the water would sink knee-deep into the slime, while the shallowness of the water would not have permitted a large man like himself to swim), it would have got dark without anything being achieved. Fortunately, however, Christodoulis, your childhood friend, lurking in the reeds, was far nearer the boat. Without a moment's hesitation and dressed in his shirt and trousers, which was all he ever wore, he unexpectedly and amazingly leapt out of the reeds like the last descendant of an ancient lake-dwelling water deity, unknown and of uncertain birth, forgotten for nineteen centuries, inhabiting the reeds and escaping the attention of the Christian world, and, throwing himself into the lagoon, began swimming. With ten strokes, his belly sometimes scraping the slimy bottom, he reached the place where the craft had got caught, sprang up

ἐπὶ τὴν δεξιὰν πλευράν, ἔδραξε τὴν πρῷραν τῆς σκάφης, καὶ μὲ ἀπίστευτον διὰ τὴν ἡλικίαν του ῥώμην, τὴν ἀνεσήκωσε καὶ τὴν ἀπήλλαξεν ἀπὸ τοῦ ἐμποδίου τῶν ὑψηλῶν χόρτων. Εἶτα ἐξέμπλεξε καὶ τὸ κοντάρι ἀπὸ τὸ μέρος ὅπου εἶχεν ἐμπλακῇ, καὶ εἶπεν εἰς τὸν Νῖκον:

— Νά, πῶς ν' ἀβαράρῃς!

Καὶ τοῦ ἔδειξεν ἐμπράκτως τὸν τρόπον, ῥίψας αὐτῷ τὸ κοντάριον.

Εἶτα ὤθησε τὴν φελούκαν ἀπὸ τῆς πρύμνης, ἀπομακρύνας αὐτὴν τῶν λιμναίων χόρτων, ὡς καὶ τῶν ῥηχῶν, ἐνῷ ἡ Πολύμνια τὸν ἐκοίταζε μειδιῶσα καὶ ἄκουσα τὸν ἐθαύμαζεν, ὑποψιθυρίζουσα:

— Τί παράξενο παιδί!

Καὶ τοὺς κατευώδωσε πρὸς τὸ μέρος τῆς καλύβης, ὅπου οἱ δύο συμπόται εἶχαν σηκωθῇ ἔκπληκτοι, μὴ ἐννοοῦντες τί συνέβαινε, καὶ ὁ Λούκας φανταζόμενος τὴν λίμνην ὡς θάλασσαν, ἔλεγε:

— Κανένα δελφίνι θὰ ἔπεσε κοντὰ στὴ βάρκα.

— Φθάνει νὰ μὴν εἶναι κανένα σκυλόψαρο, καὶ σοῦ ἀφανίσῃ τὰ κεφαλόπ'λα, καρδάσ', εἶπεν ὁ Παρρήσης.

* * *

Ὁ Χριστοδουλὴς ἐπέστρεψεν εἰς τὸν καλαμῶνά του, ὅπου, ὁ μπαρμπα-Κωνσταντὴς, αἰωνία ἡ μνήμη του, ὁ Μιτζέλος, ἀπὸ τοῦ λευκοῦ του οἰκίσκου, τοῦ γειτονεύοντος μὲ τὸν καλαμῶνα, εἶχεν ἰδεῖ τὸ συμβεβηκός, καὶ καλέσας τὸν νέον, ὅστις γυμνωθεὶς προσεπάθει νὰ στεγνώσῃ τὰ ἐνδύματά του ἐπὶ βράχου καίοντος ἀκόμη ἀπὸ τὸ καῦμα τοῦ ἄρτι δύσαντος ἡλίου, τοῦ ἔδωκεν αὐτὸς ἐνδύματα νὰ φορέσῃ. Καὶ ὁ μπαρμπα-Γιωργός, Θεὸς σχωρέσ' τον, ὁ Κοψιδάκης, ὅστις εὑρίσκετο ἐκεῖ πλησίον μὲ τὰς ὀλίγας ἀμνάδας του, τοῦ ἔδωκε «μίαν εὐχὴ» καὶ τοῦ εἶπεν ὅτι θὰ ἔχῃ «μεγάλον μισθόν», χωρὶς νὰ ὑποπτεύσῃ ὅτι αὐτὸς ἦτο νοθογενὲς ἀπότοκον λησμονημένης θεότητος. Καὶ ὁ Λούκας, μαθὼν ἐκ στόματος τῆς Πολυμνίας τὸ μικρὸν συμβεβηκός, κρατῶν εἰς χεῖρας τὴν φλάσκαν, μὲ τὰς ἀπομεινάσας ὀλίγας σταγόνας μοσχάτου, ἔκραζεν ἀπὸ τῆς ἀντιπέραν ὄχθης:

— Στὴν ὑγειά σ', Κ'στοδουλή!

* * *

Πρὸς τί νὰ χάνῃ τις τὴν φιλίαν τῶν φίλων του; Μὴ τυχὸν ἡ Πολύμνια ἦτο διὰ σὲ ἢ δι' ἐκεῖνον; Παιδίον! Αὐτὴ ἦτο μεγαλυτέρα τὴν ἡλικίαν καὶ

to the right side of the boat and, with a strength incommensurate with his age, raised it slightly, freeing it from the tall weeds. Then he disentangled the pole and said to Nikos:

'Look, this is how you punt!'

So saying, he demonstrated how it should be done, then threw the pole to Nikos. Grabbing the boat by the stern, he pushed it away from the waterweed and the shallows, while Polymnia watched him with a smile and, in involuntary admiration, whispered:

'What a strange boy!'

He swam beside them towards the hut, where the two topers were standing in amazement, wondering what was happening. Loukas, mistaking the lagoon for the sea, said:

'A dolphin must have come up to the boat.'

'As long as it's not a shark that'll eat all your mullet, friend,' said Parrisis.

* * *

Christodoulis returned to his reeds, where old Konstandis Mitzelos, of eternal memory, had witnessed the incident from his white cottage nearby; calling the young lad, who had taken his clothes off and was trying to dry them on a rock that was still burning from the heat of the sun that had just set, he gave him some clothes to put on. And old Yorgos Kopsidakis, God rest his soul, who happened to be nearby with his few ewes, gave him a blessing and assured him he would receive 'a great reward',* not suspecting that Christodoulis was the illicit fruit of the loins of a forgotten deity. And Loukas, learning about this little incident from Polymnia and holding up the flask containing a few drops of *moschato*, shouted across to the opposite bank:

'Your health, Christodoulis!'

* * *

Why should one lose the affection of one's friends? It's not as if Polymnia was destined for you or for him. Silly child! She was

τῶν δύο σας. Ἀλλὰ πῶς δύναταί τις νὰ γίνη ἀνὴρ χωρὶς ν' ἀγαπήση δεκάκις τοὐλάχιστον καὶ δεκάκις ν' ἀπατηθῇ;

Τώρα ἡ Πολύμνια ἀπέθανεν ἢ ὑπανδρεύθη; Ἀγνοῶ, ἴσως καὶ σὺ ἐπίσης. Καὶ ὁ Χριστοδουλής; Ἔγινεν ναυτικὸς περίφημος, ἀλλ' ἀπὸ ἐτῶν δὲν ἤκουσές τι περὶ αὐτοῦ. Ἴσως νὰ ἐπῆγεν εἰς τὴν Ἀμερικὴν καθὼς τόσοι ἄλλοι. Καὶ σύ; Φιλοσοφεῖς, ὡς ἐγώ, καὶ οὐδὲν πράττεις.

older than either of you. But how is one to grow to manhood without falling in love and being disappointed at least ten times?

Is Polymnia dead or married now? I don't know, and neither perhaps do you. And Christodoulis? He became a renowned sailor, but for years now you haven't heard anything about him. Perhaps he went to America, like so many others. And you? Like me, you waste your time philosophizing, and do nothing.*

Notes

and

Map of Skiathos

Page

17 A humorous variation on John 17 : 10.

19 *Bárba*: literally 'uncle', used affectionately with reference to an elderly man.

25 *Koumbáros* (m.), *koumbára* (f.), *koumbároi* (pl): a designation referring either to the godfather of a child or the best man or woman at a wedding. In Greek society the ties beween *koumbároi* are held in high esteem and considered sacred since they are sanctioned by either the sacrament of baptism or marriage.

27 Byron, *Childe Harold's Pilgrimage*, Canto IV, stanza CLXXX.

29 According to G. A. Rigas, *Skiathou laikos politismos* [*The popular culture of Skiathos*], vol. 4 (Thessaloniki, 1970), p. 279, the launching of a ship should be avoided at the solstice. Sailors believed that with every new moon a star is born which in the first two days of its existence disappears into the depths of the earth and reappears on the third day. On the day the hull of a new ship is to be built care must be taken to align the stern of the ship with the new-born star after its reappearance.

33 *Tsípouro*: a strong acoholic drink, usually disilled from the skins, seeds and stalks remaining after the grapes have been pressed for the vintage. It is also known as *rakí* and *tsikoudiá*.

35 These festivals fall on four successive days from 29 June to 2 July.

35 The island of Skopelos.

37 Cf. Sophocles, *Antigone*, 232 ('thus does a short road become long').

57 *Moscháto*: a sweet white wine made from muscat grapes.

57 *Zarar yok:* Turkish, meaning 'no harm done'.

63 See Matthew 5 : 12 and Luke 6 : 23.

65 This seems to be an ironic reference to an already humorous passage in Plato, *Symposium*, 173a, in which Apollodorus tells Glaucon that before he began keeping daily company with Socrates, 'what with running about aimlessly and thinking that I was doing something, I was the most wretched man alive, just as you are now, thinking that one should do anything rather than philosophize.'

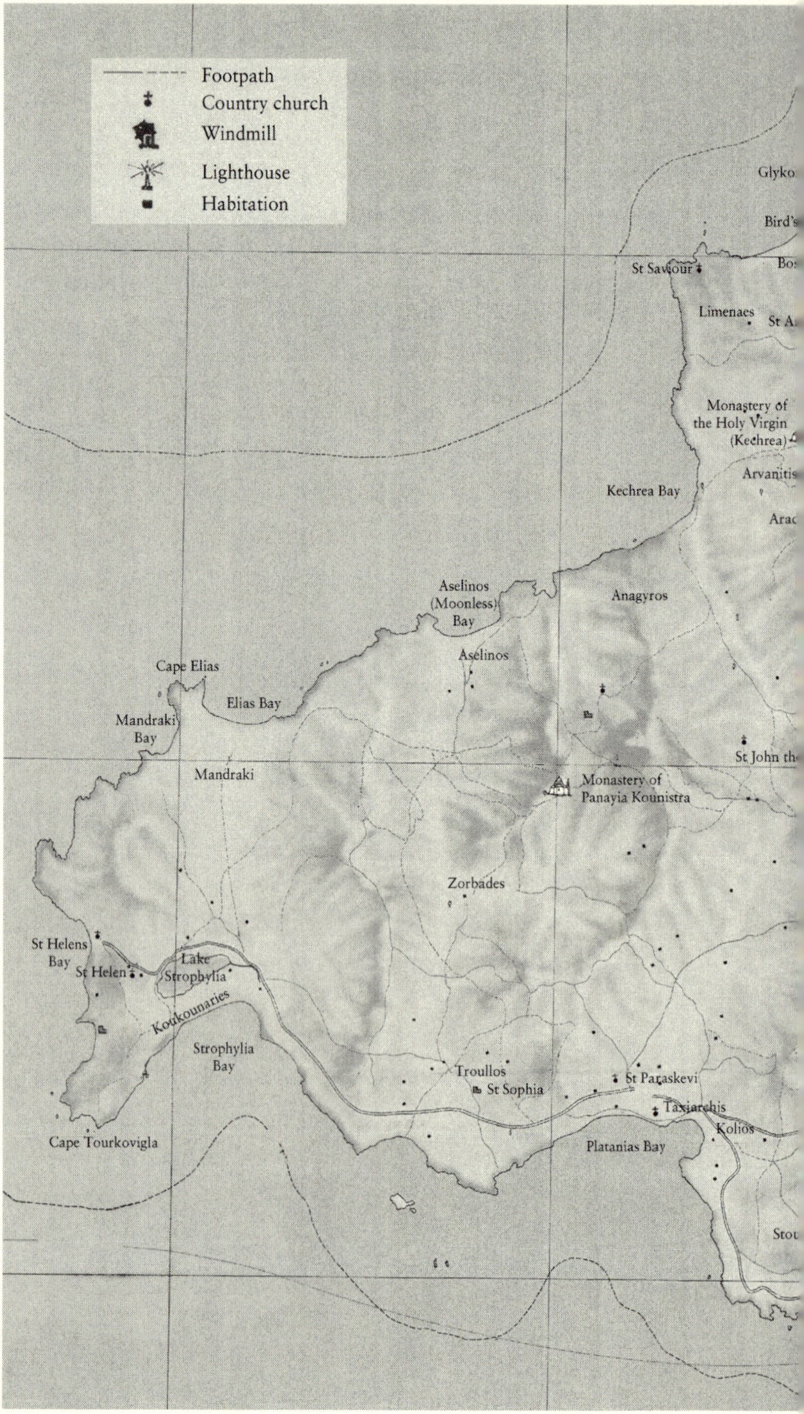
Footpath
Country church
Windmill
Lighthouse
Habitation
St Saviour
Limenaes
Monastery of
the Holy Virgin
(Kechrea)
Arvanitis
Kechrea Bay
Aselinos
(Moonless)
Bay
Anagyros
Aselinos
Cape Elias
Elias Bay
Mandraki
Bay
Mandraki
Monastery of
Panayia Kounistra
Zorbades
St Helens
Bay
St Helen
Lake
Strophylia
Koukounaries
Strophylia
Bay
Troullos
St Sophia
St Paraskevi
Taxiarchis
Kolios
Platanias Bay
Cape Tourkovigla

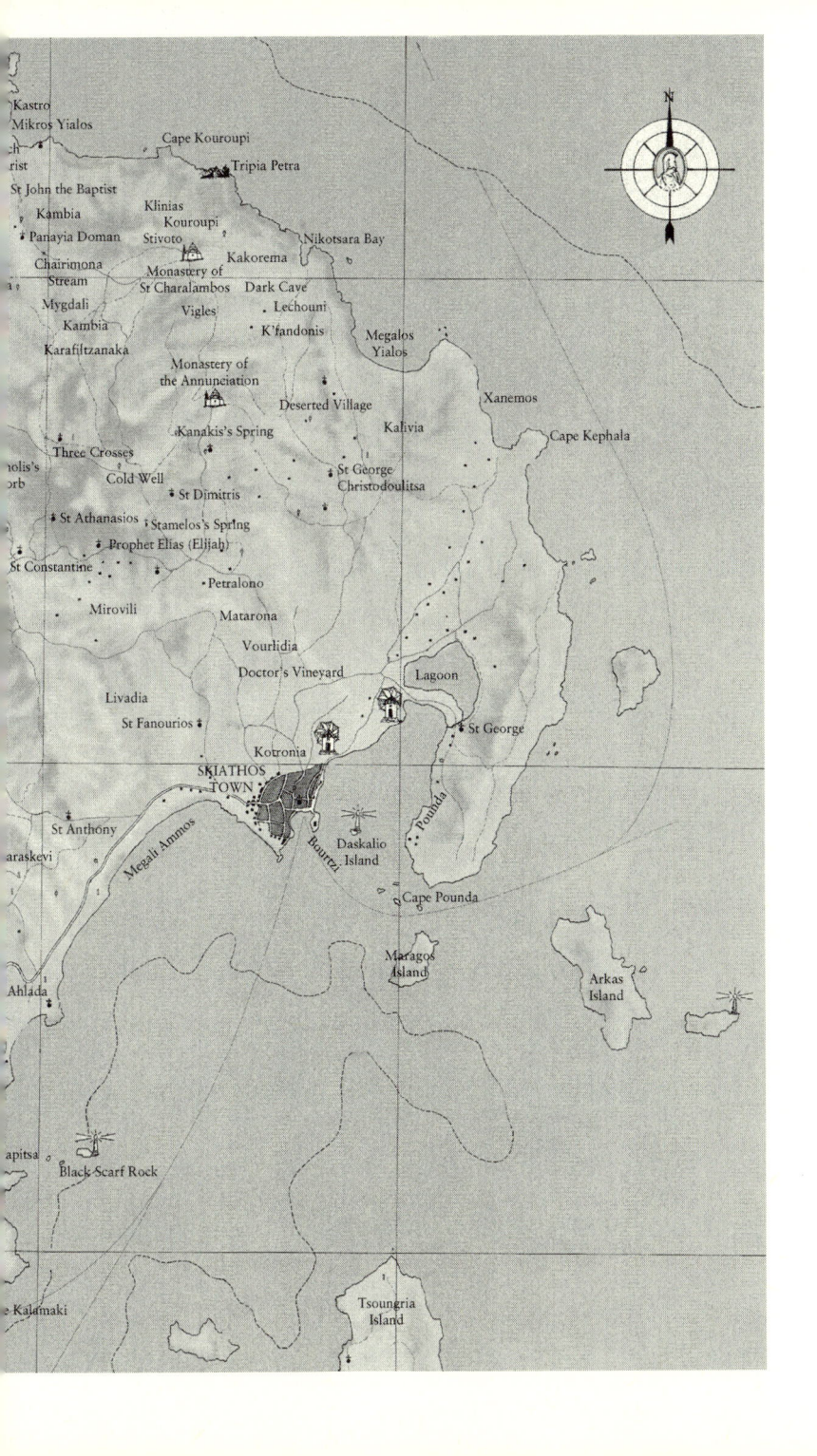

Kastro
Mikros Yialos
rist
St John the Baptist
Kambia
Panayia Doman
Chairimona
Stream
Mygdali
Kambia
Karafiltzanaka

Cape Kouroupi
Tripia Petra
Klinias
Kouroupi
Stivoto
Monastery of
St Charalambos
Vigles
Nikotsara Bay
Kakorema
Dark Cave
Lechouni
K'fandonis
Megalos
Yialos

Monastery of
the Annunciation
Kanakis's Spring
Three Crosses
Cold Well
St Dimitris
St Athanasios
Stamelos's Spring
Prophet Elias (Elijah)
St Constantine
Petralono
Mirovili
Matarona
Vourlidia
Doctor's Vineyard
Livadia
St Fanourios
Kotronia
SKIATHOS
TOWN
St Anthony
araskevi
Megali Ammos
Boureri
Deserted Village
Kalivia
St George
Christodoulitsa
Xanemos
Cape Kephala

Lagoon
St George
Pounda
Daskalio
Island
Cape Pounda

Ahlada
Maragos
Island
Arkas
Island

apitsa
Black Scarf Rock

Kalamaki
Tsoungria
Island